Budget Optimization and Allocation: An Evolutionary Computing Based Model

Authored by

Keshav Sinha

Birla Institute of Technology, Mesra, Ranchi, Jharkhand, India

Moumita Khowas

Sidho-Kanho-Birsha University, Purulia West-Bengal, India

&

Sudip Kumar Sahana

Birla Institute of Technology, Mesra, Ranchi, Jharkhand, India

General:

1. Any dispute or claim arising out of or in connection with this License Agreement or the Work (including non-contractual disputes or claims) will be governed by and construed in accordance with the laws of the U.A.E. as applied in the Emirate of Dubai. Each party agrees that the courts of the Emirate of Dubai shall have exclusive jurisdiction to settle any dispute or claim arising out of or in connection with this License Agreement or the Work (including non-contractual disputes or claims).
2. Your rights under this License Agreement will automatically terminate without notice and without the need for a court order if at any point you breach any terms of this License Agreement. In no event will any delay or failure by Bentham Science Publishers in enforcing your compliance with this License Agreement constitute a waiver of any of its rights.
3. You acknowledge that you have read this License Agreement, and agree to be bound by its terms and conditions. To the extent that any other terms and conditions presented on any website of Bentham Science Publishers conflict with, or are inconsistent with, the terms and conditions set out in this License Agreement, you acknowledge that the terms and conditions set out in this License Agreement shall prevail.

Bentham Science Publishers Ltd.
Executive Suite Y - 2
PO Box 7917, Saif Zone
Sharjah, U.A.E.
Email: subscriptions@benthamscience.org

BENTHAM SCIENCE

CONTENTS

FOREWORD

The book titled "Budget Optimization and Allocation: An Evolutionary Computing Based Model" caters to a critical need in today's intellectual landscape, *viz.*, the problem of budget optimization and distribution and its solution. The material covered in the book is an excellent balance of theory and practice. The techniques discussed the attempt to synergise evolutionary computation (mainly genetic algorithm) with traditional approaches to budget allocation like optimal allocation, equal allocation, *etc.*

The attractiveness of the book comes from the fact that it takes as a case study the complex and vast problem of union budget of India. The macro and micro issues discussed with attention to details, with the growth rate being the final aim of the budget exercise. The second attractive aspect is that the authors compare and contrast the budget allocation practices of different countries, consistent with country's economy, culture, population, *etc.* The final attractiveness is the use of very modern methodologies like evolutionary computation to tackle incremental budgeting.

This book will be found useful by graduate students in their research. I congratulate the authors on taking up a very timely and relevant problem.

Dr. Pushpak Bhattacharyya
Computer Science and Engineering,
IIT Patna,
India
and
Department of Computer Science and Engineering,
IIT Bombay,
India

PREFACE

This book builds up an innovative framework for budget optimization and allocation using Evolutionary Computing (Genetic Algorithm) in addition to conventional techniques (OCBA, EA) to get synergy from each technique.

Budget allocation plays a significant role in the planning, managing and controlling aspects of developmental processes of any given setup. Funds generated from revenue and taxes, funds collected from different agencies are essential conditions for economic growth in any country. For overall growth of a country, it is required to analyze the gain or output of the budgeting and line up the proper budgeting system. This book concentrates on the issues of good budgeting and a design a framework for proper budgeting. The chapters of the book divided into four parts:

Chapter 1 gives the introduction about the budget and its importance and challenges of budget allocation in the national and global economy. The author explains the pros and cons of budget allocation.

Chapter 2 deals with the various traditional approaches for budget allocation. Moreover, a subsequent number of researchers performed by different researchers on this topic. In depth, literature has been presented in this chapter to make a foundation for creating a research methodology on this subject.

Chapter 3 presents the proposed methodology and models for allocation and optimization. Here, Growth Rate is displayed as a parameter for allocation, explaining how evolutionary computing technology is used for optimization in this chapter.

Chapter 4 highlights the results and discussions of the different test cases of proposed budget optimization technique and allocation of the budget applied to the different schemes in the secondary education system in the MHRD department as a case study. The output of budget allocation is drawn and compared to the current budget technique.

This book is research oriented and side by side, it has practical implementation details of the research theme. Textbooks and reference books are available in the market, but that discusses only standard theories. This book is specialized and has a credit to give new ideas and implementation details in this field.

Dr. Sudip Kumar Sahana
Birla Institute of Technology, Mesra,
Ranchi, Jharkhand,
India

DEDICATION

In the loving memory of my Grand Mother Late Smt. Prabhawati Devi

This book dedicated to my Grand Father Shri. Kanhai Prasad Sinha

And to my lovely family members Mom and Dad and special thanks to my uncles

Mr. Mohan Prasad Sinha

And

Mr. Sachindra Kumar Verma

Thanks to my Special friend which has always motivated me Ms. Shweta Kumari

And Special thanks to my Guide Mr. Sudip Kumar Sahana for his support and guidance,

with which I could have never completed this book.

"If you want, then you can do it."

Keshav Sinha

SUMMARY

In daily life, the most frequently encountered problem is how to estimate expenditure. For estimation, budgeting is the best tool for determining a plan to spend money. This expense on the project is called a budget Allocation. Budget Allocation holds the planning of actual operations by handling concern problems before they arise for any private aided, government or non-government supported sectors. So, without budget allocation expenditure limits exceeded the revenue and it caused financial shortfalls. Budget information supports the planning, managing, and controlling aspects of developmental processes of any given setups. There are several conventional budget allocation and optimization techniques such as Ranking and Selection (R&S), Incremental Budgeting, Zero-Based Budgeting, Ordinary Least Square (OLS), Two-Stage Least Squares (2SLS) and Pareto Efficiency or Pareto Optimality, *etc*. But for the large-scale budgeting problem, the efficiency of conventional optimization techniques degrades. Nowadays, western countries such as USA, New Zealand, Australia, the Netherlands, Great Britain, Sweden, France, and Germany started to implement the model of Result-Oriented Budget. The concept of Result-Oriented Budgeting (ROB) is to interrelate the decisions on expenditures with the expected return of the expenses, their effectiveness, and efficiency. Concepts of the Result-Oriented Budgeting (ROB) based on the idea of the Program-Targeted Planning developed in the 1960–1970s in the USSR and the Planning-Programming-Budgeting System (PPBS) formulated in the USA in the late 1950s–early 1960s.But still, ROB has not achieved its objectives technically. Also, a lot of challenges such as policy decisions, economic crisis, inflation, public relation with neighbor countries, *etc*. have been forced to cope up with the global economy. The Chinese use the zero- based budgeting and integrated fiscal budgeting technique which is not an efficient at all. In India, there is no such protocol for budgeting policy, but uses an incremental budgeting system which lacks outcome-based approach. Finally, for all countries, specially developed and developing countries budget allocation is one of the main important concern for their growth. So, to overcome this problem, we would like to propose an Evolutionary Computing technique for budget optimization using Optimal Computing Budget Allocation Technique (OCBA), Equal Allocation (EA), and Genetic Algorithm (GA). Out of three, the two techniques were chosen for budget allocation by averaging their results which are near to the Growth Rate. The optimized budget for different schemes are allocated using ranking and selection process containing (i) 50 percent of amount using equal allocation (ii) 30 percent of a sum, according to efficiency measured from reports available from the previous year and (iii) 20 percent the fund according to the priority. The budget allocation for a department containing some schemes obtained by the cumulative sum of all projects under that department. A state or country provides some fixed number of agencies. Thus, the budget allocation for the state/country can be achieved using our proposed technique.

Keywords

Equal Allocation (EA), Genetic Algorithm (GA), Growth Rate, Optimal Computing Budget Allocation (OCBA).

CHAPTER 1

Introduction

Abstract: This chapter deals with the different budget allocation techniques used by various nations and particularly the Republic of India. Different countries used different methods of funds distributed among their several sectors. To allocate money in the budget different countries pay heed over Defense, Education, and Health Care. They provide a considerable sum of money to these three areas. Except this government employs relatively little amounts of funds in other departments. For budget allocation governments of different countries use different methods like Ranking & Selection, Incremental Budget, and Pareto Optimal. The government aims for overall better development in all aspects. The objective of this chapter is to put forward different budget allocation techniques in front of readers so that one can understand the pros and cons of a particular method and can able to use a technique for a complete budgeting problem.

Keywords: Equal Allocation (EA), Genetic Algorithm (GA), Growth Rate, Optimal Computing Budget Allocation (OCBA).

A budget is a fiscal plan which is used to estimate the revenues and expenditures for a period or time. It is just a planning tool for management [1, 2] and it assists in the allocation of resources. There are several traditional approaches for budget allocation schemes such as Ranking and Selection (R&S), Pareto Optimal, and Incremental budgeting, *etc*. Since past several years, the government used the Incremental budgeting technique where government adds a certain amount of capital to the previous year budget to allow a little increment in the budget. One of the biggest problems with this type of budgeting system is that it often leads the departments/ministries to spend more money without any result. Within this thesis, we use a modified version of the Incremental budgeting technique using OCBA and Genetic Algorithm for budget allocation.

1.1. IMPORTANCE AND CHALLENGES OF BUDGET ALLOCATION IN NATIONAL AND GLOBAL ECONOMY

Budget is a national fiscal state fund that labels the financial support for execution of its tasks and functions. Aaron B. Wildavsky's book "Budgeting: A comparative theory of budgeting processes" arises some queries like: (i) the plan of allocation, and (ii) plan to execute. The planning of the budget done according to the resources and wealth existing in every country. According to the economist, if any country is poor and the environment condition is even and firm, then the revenue budgeting is more suitable for those countries. In another case, if the country has no wealth, no environmental conditions or the environmental conditions are uncertain, then in those conditions, the repetitive budgeting is the best option. Repetitive budgeting is the most known phenomenon for the deprived countries where budgeting occurs in various intervals in the year due to fluctuating situations, restricted capitals and inappropriate schemes. The rich republic countries who have assured environments will use the incremental budgeting technique. Even though if there are uncertainties in the climate, Incremental Budget method is alternated by way of Repetitive Budgeting, which is one of the ways for the allocation of the budget. The other way is how any country chooses the tax system and how money is spent on the different schemes. In countries like Japan, the electoral party, and Liberal Democratic Party, play a huge role in the budgeting allocation. In France, there is a presidential-parliamentary system; the USA has a self-determining administration and executives, and in the UK the cabinet proceeds all responsible decisions regarding revenues, taxes, and expenditures. There are certain steps taken for budget allocation by different countries such as: In the USA, "Office of Management and Budget" steers and realizes the goals of budget. The individual government organization places their request for funds which are being dealt by the government. After that member of the House Appropriations Committee decides in what ways the fund should be given for each proposal. However, the final judgment relies within the members of congress. Since 1974, many sub committees had contributed their responsibilities for restructuring of budget, and it was taken over by the higher bodies. India is also known as a developing country where the finance ministry presents the union budget every year in the month of February. This process begins with two parts: (i) Budget Speech in the parliament on outlining the general economic scenario and (ii) Details of the projected taxations for the succeeding fiscal year. After that overall conversations on the budget occur and grant the request which is passed by voters.

A significant scenario of this process is the Cut Motion in which the upper members of the house can question on the policies and programs of the government and how much money is spent on each scheme. All the reports are sent to the standing committee and are in convincing nature (under rule 331N). And reports are not suggested for any cut motion view.

There are three types of cut motion:

1. Policy cut, where the demanded amount is reduced by an insufficient Rs.1

which also points towards disapproval of the plan.

2. Economic cut, where the particular sum reduced concerning the request.

3. Token cut, where Rs.100 reduces the amount sought.

The work of the committee is to examine the financial details thoroughly regarding government spending on the schemes and discuss the performance of the plans. In the UK, the budgetary process is a little bit longer, where each department presents its funding request to the Majesty's Treasury. Every year, government releases the supply related documents. An individual commit oversight the papers in the parliament and if there is any change made, then the request is stated. The government of the UK does not take any decision on the new budget until the next session starts, therefore, the funding related to the respective agencies is active until the new National budget is endorosed. In China, which has the fastest developing economy, the central organization known as the Ministry of Finance (MoF) controls the budget. The committee audits the MoF regarding inconsistency which is quoted by them and revises the allocation of amounts. There is a root problem in the Chinese budgeting policy where the national people's Congress is having lack of extensive control over the budgeting process, which causes the economic crisis in the country. Table **1**, shows the recent budget allocation schemes of different countries.

Table 1. Shows the Budgeting Process of Different Countries.

Country	Allocation Method	Budget Flexibility	Budget Control	Assignment Criteria of Operational Cost
Germany	Based on the Annual sum	Flexible in some particular condition	Office of State	(1) The quality of services. 2) Service Treasure. 3) Function. 4) A number of the population covered. 5) The level of duty.
Canada	Total Budget Annually (Global)	Not Flexible	State official and health ministry.	Regarding Amount estimated for the expense.
Netherland	Global	In economy issues.	By Central Government	1) Service Availability. 2) Capacity. 3) Volume Services.
Sweden	Total Budget Annually	Flexible for Patients outside limit.	District Council (Civic)	View of the district councils.
UK (United Kingdom)	Total Budget Annually (Global)	Flexible in some cases.	Regional and District health offices.	Priorities and Limitation.

(Table 1) contd.....

Country	Allocation Method	Budget Flexibility	Budget Control	Assignment Criteria of Operational Cost
Turkey	Total Budget Annually (Global)	Not Flexible	Health Ministry	Based on occurred expenditures and the price rises rate.
US (United States)	Total Budget Annually (Global)	Flexible	By federal government	Fixed mechanism is not dominant.
Australia	Total Budget Annually (Global)	Not Flexible	State Government	Find the difference based on this method.
Japan	Total Budget Annually (Global)	Not Flexible	By Government	Request rate and the government agreement.
Denmark	Total Budget Annually (Global)	Flexible	By Municipality	View of Council and Municipality.
Norway	Total Budget Annually (Global)	Flexible	By Municipality	Council and Municipality.

The study cited in Table **1**, shows that most of the countries allocate the budget annually. However, in some countries, the proposed budget is allocated in the form of fixed technique or cost recompense ways. In some countries, Flexible Budgeting changes in some conditions like monitoring and allocating of the budget differ by different governments. Anna H. Glenngard *et al.* [3], stated in the Government of Sweden where the district council is responsible for such control. In Germany, the current budget [4] is considered to allocate while distribution criteria might vary. The functioning budget allocation for hospitals in Germany requires the annual discussions with the administration ensures, disease society, private insurers and hospital legislative body at present. In the United Kingdom, the fund is allocated from the Royal Treasury in the Ministry of Health after then, it was given to local health officials after the regional health offices and finally to the hospitals. In Turkey, hospitals direct their needs at given costs and inflation rate to the provincial directors, and it is forwarded to the Ministry of Health. In the assembly, some of the requested budgets are decided by the ministry of health, and the agreed amount sent to the Parliament for approval.

In Iran, the resources allocated annually. Every country has its expenditure and the needs, and according to that the infrastructure of the budget is created. But for every infrastructure, there are certain parameters such as (i) Priorities in public, (ii) Size of the population, (iii) Population age, and (iv) The Political Environment of that country. According to these parameters, the government can spend the large part of the budget in the field of Military, Health Care, and Education Infrastructure. Here is the summary regarding how different countries spend their funds in the primary sectors like Military, Health Care and the Education.

Military

A huge part of the budget has been spent in to strengthen the power of the Military in most of the nation. In Fig. (**1**), shows that different countries allocate the percentage of the estimated amount. A recent survey tells us that Canada, spends 6.3 percent budget amount on empowerment of the military. United States (US), employ 19.3% of its budget amount for military expenditures. Mexico uses 3.3% of the estimated amount of military reinforcement. Nicaragua spends 3.2% of the yearly budget amount on the army expenses. A Country like Columbia pays 11.9% of the annual budget in the empowerment of the military. In Argentina, the government spend its 5.9% of the yearly budget for the military expenditure. In Scandinavia and Europe, governments apply a meagre amount in the armed forces expenses.

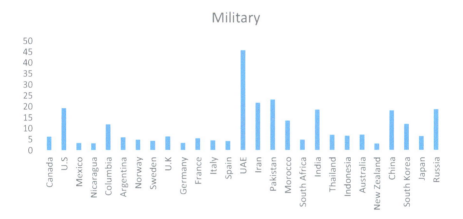

Fig. (1). Different countries spending money in the field of Military.

In Norway, 4.8% of the budget is used for military expenditure, while neighbour country Sweden spends the 4.3% of the budget on military reinforcement. U.K government pays 6.3% of the yearly budget in the armed forces. Whereas, in Germany, the 3.3% of the total amount expensed in the military. In France, 5.4% of the budget spent in the army reinforcement. In Italy, the government uses 4.5% of the annual budget for military empowerment. The annual military expenditure of Spain is 4.2%. In the Middle East countries, the military expenses are higher than in Europe. In the United Arab Emirates (UAE), the military expenditure reaches up to 45.7 percent of the country annual total budget. In Iran, the total military expenditure is 21.7% of the allocated budget. The yearly expense in Pakistan is 23.1% on the military. Morocco spends 13.6% of its total budget on the military. For the army of South Africa, the government, pays 4.8% of its budget. In the Republic of India military expenditure is 18.6 percent of its total budget. Thailand spends 7 percent of its fund on its military. Indonesia directs 6.5 percent of its budget in the armed forces expenditure. In Australia, 7.1 percent of its total budget passes on the military. In New Zealand government spends its 3.1 percent of the total amount on the military. In China, 18.2% of the annual budget given to military expenditures. South Korea spends 12% of its annual outflow on the military. In Japan, the military expenses percentage is 6.4 of the annual national budget. Russia spends 18.7% of its annual budget on military reinforcement.

Health Care

Different countries spend their enormous fund in the field of Health Care and research in the field of medicine. In Fig. (**2**), shows that the percentage of the budget allocated to the health care in a recent study.

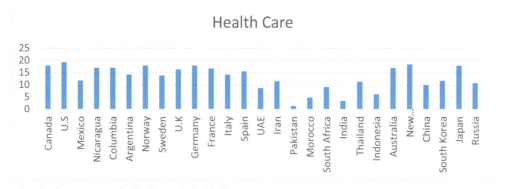

Fig. (2). Budget allocated in the field of Health Care.

Canada spends 17.9% of the budget on health care, whereas, the United States spends 19.3% of its budget on health care. Mexico and Nicaragua pay 11.8% and 17% of their total yearly budget on health care. In Columbia, health care expenditure is 17% of its annual budget. Argentina, Norway, and Sweden spend 14.2%, 17.9% and 13.8% of their yearly budget on health care. U.K and France like countries spend budget percent near about, 16.3% and 16.7% of the annual expenditure in the Health Care. In Germany, health care expense is 17.9 percent. Italy uses 14.2% of its total annual budget for health care. The annual medical expense of Spain is 15.5%. The countries like United Arab Emirates, Iran, Pakistan, and Morocco spend 8.7%, 11.5%, 1.3% and 4.8% of their annual budgets on health care expenditures respectively. The health care outflow in South Africa is 9.1% of its budget. In the Republic of India, medical expenses are 3.4% of its total budget expenditure. Thailand and Indonesia spend 11.3% and 6.2% of their funds on their health care. Australia and New Zealand spend 17%

and 18.4% of their total yearly budget on health care. In China, 9.9% of the annual budget expensed on health care. South Korea and Japan spend 11.7% and 17.9% of their total yearly expenditures on health care. Russia spends 10.8% of the annual budget on the health care.

Education

Education is the root for the growth of any developed or developing nation. Fig. (**3**), demonstrates the percentage of the annual amount spent by different countries in education infrastructure.

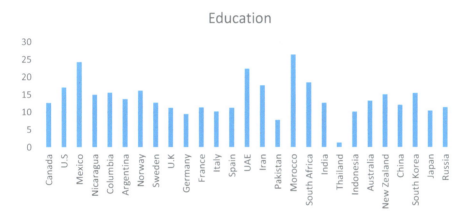

Fig. (3). Allocation of the budget in Educational Infrastructure by various Nation.

So, considering this as a parameter, different nations spend a certain percentage of the budget amount in the development of educational infrastructure. In Canada, 12.7% of its total yearly budget spends on education. Countries like the United Arab Emirates (UAE), Columbia, and Mexico spend a huge part of the budget amount in building the infrastructure of the education. A nation like Nicaragua spends 15% of its yearly budget. Argentina spends 13.8% on education annually. Norway employs 16.2% of its budget on education while Sweden fills 12.8% of its budget in education. The U.K. government uses 11.5% on education yearly. Germany and France, spend 9.5% and 11.4% annually on education. Italy and Spain use 10.3% and 11.3% of its annual budget for building the school infrastructure. Muslim countries like Iran, Pakistan, and Morocco spend 17.7%, 7.8% and 26.4% of the budget amount yearly. South Africa employs 18.5% of the budget on education. In the Republic of India, expenses rise to 12.7% of the budgeted amount on education infrastructure. Thailand passes 14% on education. Australia and New Zealand give 13.3% and 15.1% of their yearly budget on education. The super power nations like the United States (US), China, South

Korea and Japan spend 16.6%, 12.1%, 15.5% and 10.5% of the annual budget on education respectively. Russia spends 11.5% of its yearly budget on the school infrastructure. So, according to this parameter Budget is a national fiscal state fund that labelled the financial support for execution of its tasks and functions. The state puts onward the work of formation of a program-based directed control of budget funds with an account for urgencies of socioeconomic development of the country. For the various economic development of the state, the problem of allocation of budgetary resources is one of the main tasks of the financial processes. The state, country and global economic problem as a subject of control act as the force of amalgamation, assistance, and combination. Therefore, an equal role in the macroeconomic process is played by the budget a federal monetary fund that acts as an object, adaptable to state financial fund. Its role is to observe and control the development of the country.

1.2. ADVANTAGES AND DISADVANTAGES OF BUDGET ALLOCATION

There are several benefits, and drawbacks of budget allocation described below:

1.2.1. Benefits of Budget Allocation

1. The budget permits repeatedly use and save our time and efforts when put it on unique finance programs.
2. The budget provides an asset to observe the schemes and economic events over the life of the project.
3. A budget provides an outline for expenses to accomplish the purposes of the project in an efficient and optimized manner.
4. Careful supply organization will decrease the quantity variance of the budget during the whole generation of the project.

1.2.2. Disadvantage of Budget Allocation

1. The training of budgets, cost, time, and money incurred have a downfall.
2. A budget approximates the project overheads. It is never exact and therefore it can carry difficulties during the execution phase.
3. Poor monetary planning can lead to budget limitations in the center of procedures and even in complete termination.
4. Impractical budget plan causes disappointment and setback on administrative support.

CONCLUDING REMARKS

A proper budget allocation is one of the gravest concern for the growth of any developing nation. Different budget allocation schemes like Ranking & Selection,

Incremental Budget, Pareto Optimal, *etc*. are used by the various organizations for their overall better development. In this different chapter budget allocation techniques have been discussed to understand the pros and cons of a method and can able to use a technique for a complete budgeting problem.

CONSENT FOR PUBLICATION

Not applicable.

CONFLICT OF INTEREST

This presentation certify that authors have no affiliations with or involvement in any organization or entity with any financial interest (such as honoraria, educational grants, participation in speakers' bureaus, membership, employment, consultancies, stock ownership, or other equity interest; and expert testimony or patent-licensing arrangements), or nonfinancial interest (such as personal or professional relationships, affiliations, knowledge or beliefs) in the subject matter or materials discussed in this manuscript.

ACKNOWLEDGEMENTS

We would also like to thank Ms. Annu Priya, Department of Computer Science and Engineering, B.I.T. Mesra, Ranchi, for encouragement and help us to work on this topic. Without her support and vision, we couldn't complete this chapter. We also like to thank our Institute Birla Institute of Technology, Mesra, and SKBU, Purulia for supporting us with its vast collection of books in the library.

Finally, we like to acknowledge and thankful to the publisher of this book "Bentham Publisher" for its wide circulation and make a provision to reach this article to some readers.

REFERENCES

[1]   M. Karan, R. Haas, and T. Walker, "Illustration of pavement management: From data inventory to priority analysis", *Transport. Res. Board Res. Rec.,* vol. 814, pp. 22-28, 1981.

[2]   S. Kikukawa, and R. Haas, "Priority programming for network level pavement management", In: *Proceedings of Paving in Cold Areas* Tsukuba: Japan, 1984.

[3]   A.H. Glenngard, F. Hjalte, M. Svensson, A. Anell, and V. Bankauskaite, "Health Systems in Transition", *Health Syst. Transit.,* vol. 7, no. 4, 2005.

[4]   R. Busse, and A. Riesborg, "Health care system in transition." Copenhagen, "Who regional Offices for Europe on Behalf of the European Observatory on Health Systems and Policies", *Germany,* vol. 6, no. 9, 2004.

CHAPTER 2

Literature Review

Abstract: In this chapter, a detailed study has been conducted on the available literature and the work done by the different researchers. As per the available literature, many ways are available to allocate budget. The famous traditional budgeting approaches are: Zero-based Budgeting, Ordinary Least Squares Technique (OLST), and Two-stage Least Squares (2SLST). Along with the traditional approaches, Evolutionary Approach (EA) such as Optimal Computing Budget Allocation (OCBA) and Genetic Algorithm (GA) are most popular budget allocation methods in research community nowadays. So, we will discuss the glint of different observations presented in research papers. After in-depth analysis, we conclude that use of traditional budget allocation methods along with the Evolutionary Budget Allocation methods can provide a better budget allocation model and it will be exemplary for the government to make the budget for the welfare of the country. Lots of research papers have been referred as it is cited in the reference section.

Keywords: Genetic Algorithm (GA), Incremental Budgeting, Ordinary Least Squares Technique (OLST), Optimal Computing Budget Allocation (OCBA), Pareto Optimality, Ranking and Selection, Two-stage Least Squares (2SLST), Zero-based Budgeting.

Before describing the research design, it will be appropriate to explain the various techniques related to budget allocation for the sake of better and easier understanding.

2.1. TRADITIONAL BUDGET ALLOCATION TECHNIQUE

There are several conventional techniques for budget allocation. Out of them, the well-known techniques and their advancements in this direction are described below:

2.1.1. Rank and Selection Technique

Jean D *et al.* [1], introduced the ranking and selection method for searching in sample space using binomial and normal distribution. Many researchers follow this approach for searching. J. Pichitlamken [2], introduced a searching algorithm which runs on a probable set of solutions after an initial optimization for selecting the best option from the finite round of solutions from the sample space. For selection processes they are considered as π_i to denote the solution 'I' were, I = [1, 2… k]. From the observations, they have taken π_i, X_{ip}, normally distributed with mean μ_i and variance σ_i^2, where mean and variance are not necessarily equal for different solutions. So, for selecting the average of the solutions with a loss of the generality is shown in equation (1):

$$\mu_1 \leq \mu_2 \leq \ldots\ldots \leq \mu_k \tag{1}$$

In the traditional approach, for finding the best solution, the best way is to find the largest mean, which is μ_K in the current problem. In equation (2), it is shown that selecting the π_K with probability 1-α, whenever the difference between the best and the next best solution is detected as:

$$\Pr \{\text{select } \pi_k\} \geq 1\text{-}\alpha \text{ whenever } \mu_k - \mu_{k-1} \geq \delta \tag{2}$$

For supporting this feature, it is needed to set up the simulation process such that one can run the remaining replication processes for the particular solution. In simulation process, first the random seed value is set up for running additional replication process and to create the new solution for new results. The Ranking and Selection Algorithm allows us to eliminate the solutions from the candidate list until a defined number of percent chance is achieved, thus making the remaining candidates a part of the indifference zone.

2.1.2. Incremental Budgeting Technique

One of the most common methodologies for preparing the budget is incremental budgeting. It starts with taking the previous year's expenditures as an estimated expense for the current fiscal year expense. The small changes made by adding or subtracting the price in the budget shows a fluctuation in upcoming fiscal year. This type of budgeting system is the best allocation technique for large organizations with a requirement of little fluctuation.

Many government and private aided educational institutions and organizations that have the long-term funded projects use incremental budgeting. Budget line technique is used for calculating the percentage increase and decrease in the expenses. It is common for all types of organization or national resources for allocating the funds to the different ministries.

The Advantages of Incremental Budgeting Are

- Incremental budgeting is easy to implement, and it does not involve any complex calculations.
- Incremental budgeting confirms stability in capital for each department without much in-depth investigation of capital constraint.
- Incremental budgeting ensures that no huge ups and downs occur in the budget. With this type of planning, it provides stability in budgets year after year.
- Many private sectors use incremental budgeting technique to eliminate the opposition and build the value of equality.
- Incremental budgeting is very reliable for companies whose funding requirements are usually static or with very slight deviation.
- The influence of the modification in the budget is observed immediately in the case of incremental budgeting.
- It is easy to understand and the calculations are relatively straightforward.

The Disadvantages of Incremental Budgeting Are

- Incremental Budgeting assumes only those requirements which are slightly different from the preceding year.
- If there are significant structural changes concerning a private sector economy, it may permit much more substantial budget changes.
- This approach is beneficial to manage and lead to stop the un-necessary spending of funds.
- This method brings the small modification in the budget of the last year and the rest of the things remain same. It causes the lack of innovation and interaction and will not be able to reduce the cost.
- A scenario created by an incremental budgeting method is called as "Budgetary Slack" where the manager has to build the weak revenue growth and higher expense growth for favorable variances.
- Incremental budgeting can do continuous resource allocation for individual departments, even though it will not require any amount in later years.
- A similar allocation of the fund will cause the wastage of resources.

An Incremental Budgeting technique uses resource allocations based on the existing pattern of activities.

2.1.3. Zero-based Budgeting Technique

It is a decision and planning approach that reverses the working process of incremental budgeting. In traditional Incremental budgeting technique, the higher authorities of any government or private person justify the budget that is based on the assumption of the past year and budget baseline. But in the Zero-based budgeting technique, if there are some small changes in the budget base line, then it must be approved. In zero-based budget, the request is re-evaluated and starts from the zero-base. It involves preparation of a fresh budget every year without referencing the past. It is an independent process. The total amount or specific baseline items will not affect the total sum even if they increase or decrease.

2.1.4. Ordinary Least Squares Technique (OLST)

In 1962, the Arthur Melvin Okun first proposed the relationship between GDP growth and the unemployment rate. It is a method for estimating the unknown parameters in a linear regression model, with the goal of minimizing the differences between the observed responses in some arbitrary data set. If differences are smaller then, the better model fits the data. Assuming that the data is consisting of 'n' observations $\left(y_p\, x_i\right)_{i=1}^{n}$, each observation includes a scalar response 'y_i' and a vector of 'p' predictors or regressors 'x_i' then the linear regression model for response variable is shown in equation 3:

$$y_i = x_i^T \beta + \varepsilon_i \tag{2}$$

Whereas:

β = p x 1 vector.

ε_i = unobserved scalar random variables.

T= matrix transpose.

The discrepancy between the observed response y_i and the predicted outcome x_i is denoted as $x_i^T \beta$. The dot product between x and β is shown in equation 4.

$$y = X \beta + \varepsilon \tag{4}$$

Whereas:

y and ε = (n × 1) vectors.

X = n × p matrix regressors, which is also called design Matrix.

2.1.5. Two-stage Least Squares Technique (2SLST)

Two-stage least squares technique (TSLS) is used for finding the dissimilarity in variables using the regression. The name suggests that, there are two different types of stages. In the first stage, TSLS is used for finding out the portions of the indigenous and exogenous variables. It means that the value is similar but not close to the dependent variables and the variables are not affected by the other variables in the system. This stage contains approximation of variables in OLS regression model. In the second stage, the regression of the original equation variables is replaced by the fitted values of the first stage regressions. The coefficients of this two regressions are called the TSLS estimates. To represent the TSLS, we first represent the 'Z' matrix. Assuming that, 'y' and 'X' be the dependent variables, the linear TSLS objective function is given in equation 5 and 6:

$$\Psi\,(\beta) = (y - X\beta)\ ' \ Z\,(Z'Z)^{-1}\,Z'(y\text{-}X\beta) \qquad\qquad (5)$$

Then the coefficient computed in TSLS is given by:

$$b_{TSLS} = (X'Z\,(Z'Z)^{-1}\,Z'X)^{-1}\,X'Z\,(Z'Z)^{-1}\,Z'y \qquad\qquad (6)$$

The estimated covariance matrix is specified as:

$$\sum TSLS = S^2\,(X'Z\,(Z'Z)^{-1}\,Z'\,X)^{-1} \qquad\qquad (7)$$

Whereas, S^2 is the estimated residual variance or square of standard error regression.

The Regression analysis technique is used for analyzing the structural equations and also for an extension of the OLST method. Here, the errors are correlated [3] with the independent variables.

It is handy when there are feedback loops in the model. In 2SLST equation modeling, we maximize the likelihood and estimate the path of the coefficient. This technique has the substitute in structural equation modeling to approximate the path coefficient, and it is also applied in quasi-experimental setups.

2.2. LINEAR OPTIMIZATION

Linear optimization (LP) is a Mathematical Model which determines the problems of unusual resources. LP uses the objective function and the constraints of linear variables for optimization. Different researchers propose different ways for linear programming. In the year 1762, Lagrange introduced the tractable optimization problems that consist of equality constraints. In the year 1820, Gauss introduced the Gaussian elimination for the linear equation and optimization. Wilhelm, Jordan in the year 1866, suggested the modification of Least Squared Error (LSE) as a measure of goodness-of-fit. Nowadays, that equation is mentioned as a Gauss-Jordan Method. In the year 1968, Fiasco and McCormick presented the Interior Point Method for solving the linear and nonlinear convex optimization problems. Narendra Karmarkar in 1984, announced the Karmarkar's algorithm for solving linear programming problems in polynomial time. After a brief review, we can conclude that LP is the most applicable mathematical theory for modelling the problems of the real world. But there are many interesting optimization problems that are nonlinear. So, to understand those issues, the combination of linear algebra, multivariate calculus, numerical analysis, and computing techniques is needed. The various innovative areas of the computational algorithm involve the design of an interior point method like linear programming, geometry of convex sets and functions, and a unique structured problem such as quadratic programming. The nonlinear optimization delivers the essential feature in the mathematical models, and it is commonly used in the field of engineering science, regressive models, inventory structure, geophysics examination, and economic science. The objective function maps the feasible region as an input domain in an output range, and the values of the two ends are called maximum and minimum. For discussion making problems there are particular conditions such as:

i. The functions are in the linear form, and the power of the variable is '1'. They are either additive or subtractive in nature but cannot be divided or multiplied.
ii. The function must maximize or minimize, and it must represent the objective of the decision-maker.
iii. The constraints of the linear equation must be in the form of ($\geq$, $\leq$, or =).

2.3. NONLINEAR OPTIMIZATION

Nonlinear optimization is a method for solving the qualities and dissimilarities of the equation regarding constraints for unknown real variables. The constraint for the objective function is nonlinear. The subfields of the rule are also nonlinear. In non-convex problems, the transportation cost of a set of methods display the economic scale in the various capacities of constraints. In general, the nonlinear optimization is used to minimize the scale of nonlinear programming function 'f' and variables 'x,'. The limits are used to define the constraint.

In mathematical terms,

Minimize $f(x)$

Subject to $C_i(x) = 0 \ \forall i \in \varepsilon$

$C_i(x) \leq 0 \ \forall i \in I$

Whereas,

$c_i(x) = R_n$ to R_m

ε and I = index sets for equality and inequality constraints, respectively.

An equivalent formulation is:

Minimize $f(x)$

Subject to $c(x) = 0$

$L \leq x \leq u$

Whereas, c(x) maps R_n to R_m and the lower and upper bound vectors, 'L' and 'u' contain infinite components.

Nonlinear programming is a vast field containing many well-studied subfields. In general, nonlinear problems find the best solution in all such minima. In exceptional cases, the nonlinear programming is convex in nature where all the local solutions become global solutions.

2.4. METAHEURISTIC OPTIMIZATION

2.4.1. Pareto Efficiency or Pareto Optimality

Pareto efficiency or Pareto optimality is a theory of economics, but mostly the applications are in the field of engineering and social sciences. The term was named after Italian economist Vilfredo Pareto (1848-1923), whose concept is widely used in the studies of economic efficiency and distribution. Pareto Efficiency [4] is a method which deals with the system of "no allocation completed without making at least one single worse off". There is a primary distribution of goods among the set of individuals, and there is a change in an allocation that makes, at least one individual enhance without making any other individual inferior is called a Pareto improvement. An allocation can be defined as a Pareto Efficient or Pareto Optimal when there are no further developments made. Pareto efficiency has a minimal concept and does not fundamentally result in a social distribution of resources. It doesn't make any statement about equality and overall well-being of the society. Pareto's concept of extreme social welfare is based on the ordinal utility and also permitted from decisions. Pareto Optimum is impossible to make anybody wealthy without making somebody poorer by any reorganization of resources of inputs and outputs. According to Pareto optimum, the welfare of the individual cannot improve without decreasing the performance of the member. Pareto's measure for social welfare states of any restructuring economic resources which do not damage anyone and make somebody better off, then it indicates the increase in social welfare.

Marginal Conditions of Pareto Optimality

Each has its ordinal utility function and possesses a defined product and factor.

- The production function of every firm and the state of the technology are shown and remain constant.
- Goods are in the flawless divisibility.
- A manufacturer tries to produce a given output with a minimum rate of combination factors.
- Every individual wants to make the most of his fulfillment.
- Every person obtains the same capacity of all goods.
- All factors of the manufacturers are without a glitch.

Pareto Efficiency in Social welfare

Optimal distribution of the product to the consumer:

- The Marginal rate of one right for another which pays off in the marginal unit of another to maintain the continuous level of fulfillment.
- The marginal rate between two goods must be similar for any individual who consumes them both.
- If the marginal rates between two goods are not equal and when they go for an exchange, they will increase the fulfillment of both the consumers or increase one's satisfaction without upsetting the other.
- In the manufacture of different goods, it is unbearable to increase the output production of one item without decreasing the production of the other item. It is impossible for any manufacturer to reallocate the output of both the items with production.
- The production efficiency is related to the consumer preference and the technical condition for the production.
- The state of satisfaction determines when the optimal amounts of different merchandise are created with same benefaction factors.

2.4.2. Optimal Computing Budget Allocation (OCBA)

In the mid-1990s, Dr. Chun Hung Chen [5] first introduced the concept of the OCBA. This technique is used for maximizing the overall simulation efficiency for finding an optimal solution. OCBA is the simulation tactic that will help us to determine the number of replications or the simulation time needed to receive the acceptable best results within a set of given parameters. It is accomplished by using an asymptotic framework to analyze the structure of the optimal allocation. The OCBA's goal is to provide an efficient methodology [6] to run many simulations, including only the dangerous replacements to select the best alternative. In other words, the most critical option is to minimize the computation time and to reduce these chief estimator's variance. The expected result maintains the required level of accuracy while requiring less amount of work. The primary objective of OCBA is to maximize the Probability of Correct Selection (PCS). PCS is subjected to the sampling budget of a given stage of sampling as it is shown in equation (8).

$$\max_{t_1, t_2, \ldots, t_k} PCS \tag{8}$$

Whereas:

$\sum_{i=1}^{k} T_i \geq 0$, Stands for the computational cost.

Some of the traditional approaches for budget allocation are highlighted in the above sections. Apart from these, there may be possible soft computing based budget allocation techniques such as Genetic Algorithm, PSO, *etc.* Here we have mainly focused on genetic algorithm based on budget allocation. Soft computing approaches are presently one of the most advanced methodologies with ongoing research to resolve the problems automatically rather than sequentially.

Table **2** shows that the allocation of the fund in the scheme of MDM under MHRD department where every year a huge amount of money are spent for the improvement of the education sector. But there is a justified question on the amount of allocation and its efficacy. The traditional approach has a problem with distribution and optimization.

Table 2. Amount allocated in MDM under MHRD Department.

Year Wise Outlay under Midday Meal Scheme (Rs. In Crores)	
Year	Budget
2007-08	7324
2008-09	8000
2009-10	8000

(Table 2) contd.....

Year Wise Outlay under Midday Meal Scheme (Rs. In Crores)	
Year	Budget
2010-11	9440
2011-12	10380
2012-13	11937
2013-14	13215

2.4.3. Genetic Algorithm (GA)

Genetic Algorithm (GA) was firstly introduced by Holland in 1950. GA is used to mimic the processes of natural evolution and selection. Besides Genetic Programming (GP), Genetic Algorithm (GA) [7 - 9] is an evolutionary approach to resolve optimization. In this environment, every species need to adapt a challenging and varying environment to maximize the survival. Species improvement is encoded in chromosomes and transforms when reproduction occurs.

Over a period, these changes in chromosomes help the species to survive. Improved characteristics are passed to future generation, although all changes are not beneficial. Holland's genetic algorithm tries to simulate nature's algorithm in the following manner. First, the problem with a string of genes is represented, representing possible solutions known as chromosomes. Then the population of chromosomes is constructed randomly. Chromosome fitness in population is measured in each generation and to produce offspring for the next generation. After crosover, the best characteristics of both the parents were inherited. The genetic algorithm consists of following important components shown in Fig. (4):

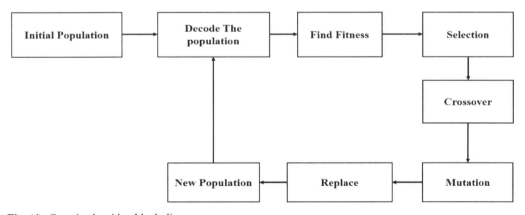

Fig. (4). Genetic algorithm block diagram.

a. **Chromosomal Representation**: Every chromosome signifies a solution to the problem and is composed of a string of genes. For representation of genes, binary alphabets [0, 1] are used, but sometimes real number or integers are used depending on the application.

b. **Initial Population:** Suitable representation is decided for chromosomes. It is necessary to create an initial population that serves as a string for a genetic algorithm. The original population is generated randomly. From the studies on full range function optimization issues, a size of population in between 30 and 100 is usually recommended but certainly depends on the applications.

c. **Fitness Evaluation:** Fitness assessment defines the fitness of chromosomes. When the algorithm proceeds, the best chromosome is selected from the whole population, and is tested in the environment.

d. **Selection:** In this process, chromosomes are selected from the reproduction. Selection procedure selects two parent chromosomes from the population based on their values of fitness which are used by crossover and mutation operators to generate two offsprings for the new population. This cycle repeats till the population attains new chromosomes.

e. **Crossover and Mutation:** Crossover is a genetic operator used to vary the programming of chromosomes from one generation to the next. A crossover is a process of taking more than one parent's solutions and producing a child's solution from them. There are different types of crossovers like a single point, two points, uniform, three parents, *etc.* Mutation maintains genetic diversity from one generation to the next. Mutation alters one or more gene values in a chromosome from its initial state. The mutation occurs during evolution according to a user-definable mutation probability. This expectation should be set low. If it is set too high, the search will turn into a fast random search.

2.5. LITERATURE SURVEY

There are several methods used for budget allocation and optimization. Among these, some of the methods are popular in the research community for optimally allocating the budget. The methods like ranking and selection have been successfully used by the simulation replication to select the best design in a subset of 'n' alternatives. The OCBA approach can intelligently determine the number of simulated replications in a set of all simulated options. However, the most real-life systems and designs have multi-objectives. Pareto optimality is a state-of-art technique, in which we cannot make any individual better without making the other worse. But different approaches have various problems like: (i) How to allocate replications to unique designs, and (ii) Multi-objective ranking and selection (MORS) problem. Lots of quality works have been performed by different researchers for budget allocation and optimization for better allocation of budget. Jian Hu *et al.* [10], introduced a model for multi-criteria, budget allocation problems under uncertainity. The changes are incorporated with decision maker's weights using a robust weighted sum approach. The author used the Average Approximation approach with the cutting-edge methods. Junqi Zhang [11], introduced the learning automation (LA) technique for reinforcement learning.

In LA, the action probability vector plays an important role in deciding the convergence of total computing budget. Optimal computing budget allocation is achieved to allocate the overall computing budget in a way so that it maximizes the probability of identifying the actual optimal actions using ε-optimality. Wai Peng Wong [12] studied that, how to allocate the budget for data collection efficiently when data envelopment analysis (DEA) was used for predicting the efficiency. They use the Bayesian framework and heuristic algorithm approach such as gradient-based algorithm and a hybrid GA algorithm to solve this optimization problem. Mark W. Brantley *et al.* [13], introduced the Ranking & Selection (R&S) procedures to enhance the simulation efficiency of finding the best design. The underlying function is optimized in one-dimensional as well as approximately quadratic or piecewise quadratic. He showed that R&S method may obtain significant savings over regression based methods. Chen [14] proposed the discrete event dynamic systems (DEDS's) simulation technique in which it provides noise performance evaluation for allocating the computing budget among different action candidates so that a better policy could be obtained with high probability. Finally, the numerical result shows that limited computing budget to allocate using OCBA-based allocation procedure outperforms equal allocation. Keshav *et al.* [15], proposed an optimal computing budget allocation (OCBA) algorithm for selecting a subset of designs for the small computing budget. Loo Hay Lee *et al.* [16, 17], applied the ranking and selection technique for identifying the best system design from a set of competing models. They have proposed the multi-objective ranking and selection problem where the system models are evaluated regarding performance measures. As per their computational results, the algorithm was efficient on the basis of the total number of replications needed to find the pareto set. A subsequent number of researches have been performed on this topic as cited below in Table **3**.

Table 3. A Summary of historical research development in this field shown below.

Research	Technique Used	Methodology	Advantages	Disadvantages
Bechhofer *et al.* [18], Swisher *et al.* [19], Kim and Nelson [20]	Indifference Zone (IZ)	Selection is guaranteed, and it selects the best design among other designs.	Increase in accuracy	Replication is present there.

(Table 3) contd.....

Research	Technique Used	Methodology	Advantages	Disadvantages
Rinott [21]	Two Stages – IZ	Selecting the best design for a single performance and in the second Stage,replication is allocated based on variance.	Improve the probability of correct selection.	Replication Allocation.
Chen *et al.* [22, 23]	Applicability of OCBA	Allocation rule in finding the optimal subset instead of single best design.	Increase in efficiency.	Less performance in the Multi objective.
Lee *et al.* [24]	Multi objective OCBA	Minimize the resources idle time. And selection of alternatives with high waiting time.	Performance increased.	Scheduling is the biggest challenge.
Davis [25]	GA	The binary encoding scheme for fitness function.	It provides flexibility.	Layout Problem, Optimization problem.
Hussein Al-Battaineh and S. AbouRizk [26]	GA_OCBA	Chromosome Encoding.	Multiplication problem solving.	No assurance of finding the global Best.
Rubinstein and Shapiro [27]	Stochastic approximation	Estimated by noisy observation.	Maximize the exception.	Unreliable stopping criteria.
Kennedy and Eberhart [28]	PSO	Decision making, using neighbors' experiences.	Robust and Easy implementation.	Replication.
Stern and Price [29]	Differential Evolution	Random searches in the solution space.	Random Search.	Unstable convergence.
Zhang *et al.* [30]	PSObw_OCBA PSOs_OCBA	Maximize the convergence rate and Probability of correct selection.	Improve the computational efficiency.	Replication.

2.6. PROBLEM STATEMENT

For budget allocation, some questions need to be solved for proper budgeting:

   i. What is significant budget?
  ii. Which type of income and expenditure pattern needs to be followed?
 iii. Scheme objectives, Scheme outcomes, Budgeting potentiality for systems, Lifetime of plans and Effectiveness of programs related to Budget.

In this book, we shall explore the research work on budget allocation process for the complete budget in an efficient manner and optimized way. A huge amount of money is spent every year on various projects, but the outcome is not as expected.

It has also been observed that the money allocated by the Government in a particular scheme is more than the consumption ability of that scheme and the output is less. So there is a huge requirement to set up a proper budgeting plan. In this book, our aim is to establish a better budget allocation system.

CONCLUDING REMARKS

Traditional approaches to Zero-based Budgeting, Ordinary Least Squares Technique (OLST), and Two-stage Least Squares (2SLST) are still in use. But Evolutionary Approach (EA) such as Optimal Computing Budget Allocation (OCBA) and Genetic Algorithm (GA) are the most popular budget allocation methods in research community nowadays. A lot of investigations have been performed by different researchers in favor of these approaches. The essence of Traditional budget allocation methods along with Evolutionary Budget Allocation methods may provide a better budget allocation model.

CONSENT FOR PUBLICATION

Not applicable.

CONFLICT OF INTEREST

This presentation certifies that authors have no affiliations with or involvement in any organization or entity with any financial interest (such as honoraria, educational grants, participation in speakers' bureaus, membership, employment, consultancies, stock ownership, or other equity interest; and expert testimony or patent-licensing arrangements), or Non-financial interest (such as personal or professional relationships, affiliations, knowledge or beliefs) in the subject matter or materials discussed in this manuscript.

ACKNOWLEDGEMENTS

We would like to thank faculty members of Department of CSE, BIT, Mesra and Dr. Suprabhat Bagli, Dept. of Economics, SKBU, Purulia for their great support to build up this chapter. We also like to thank Birla Institute of Technology, Mesra, and SKBU, Purulia for helping us with his enormous collection of books in the library.

Finally, we like to acknowledge and thankful to the publisher of this book "Bentham Publisher" for its wide circulation and make a provision to reach this article to some readers.

REFERENCES

[1]   J.D. Gibbons, I. Olkin, and M. Sobel, "An introduction to ranking and selection", *Am. Stat.,* vol. 33,

no. 4, 1979.

[2] J. Pichitlamken, and B.L. Nelson, "Selection-of-the-best procedure for Optimization *via* Simulation", *Winter Simulation Conference,* 2001

[3] M.C. Fu, J.H. Hu, C.H. Chen, and X. Xiong, "Simulation allocation for determining the best design in the presence of correlated sampling", *INFORMS J. Comput.,* vol. 19, pp. 101-111, 2007. [http://dx.doi.org/10.1287/ijoc.1050.0141]

[4] B.P. Brownstein, "Pareto optimality, external benefits, and public goods: A subjectivist approach", *J. Libert. Stud.,* vol. 4, no. 1, 1980.

[5] C.H. Chen, D. He, M. Fu, and L.H. Lee, "Efficient Simulation Budget Allocation for Selecting an optimal subset", *INFORMS J. Comput.,* vol. 20, no. 4, pp. 579-595, 2008. [http://dx.doi.org/10.1287/ijoc.1080.0268]

[6] Q.S. Jia, "Efficient computing budget allocation for simulation-based policy improvement", *Proceedings of 8th Asian Control Conference (ASCC) Kaohsiung.* [http://dx.doi.org/10.1109/TASE.2011.2181164]

[7] S.K. Sahana, and A. Jain, "An improved modular hybrid ant colony approach for solving traveling salesman problem", *Int. J. Comput.,* vol. 1, no. 2, pp. 123-127, 2011. [JoC].

[8] S.K. Sahana, A. Jain, and P.K. Mahanti, "Ant colony optimization for train scheduling: analysis", *I.J. Intel. Syst. Appl.,* vol. 6, no. 2, pp. 29-36, 2014. [http://dx.doi.org/10.5815/ijisa.2014.02.04]

[9] S. Srivastava, S.K. Sahana, D. Pant, and P.K. Mahanti, "Hybrid microscopic discrete evolutionary model for traffic signal optimization", *J. Next Gener. Informat. Technol.,* vol. 6, no. 2, pp. 1-6, 2015. [JNIT].

[10] J. Hu, T. Homem-de-Mello, and S. Mehrotra, "Risk adjusted budget allocation models with application in homeland security", *Taylor & Francis IIE Transactions,* February 2011. [http://dx.doi.org/10.1080/0740817X.2011.578610]

[11] J. Zhang, C. Wang, D. Zang, and M. Zhou, "Incorporation of optimal computing budget allocation for ordinal optimization into learning automata", *IEEE Trans. Autom. Sci. Eng.,* pp. 1545-5955, 2015.

[12] W.P. Wong, W. Jaruphongsa, and L.H. Lee, "Budget allocation for efficient data collection in predicting an accurate idea efficiency score", *IEEE Trans. Automat. Contr.,* vol. 56, no. 6, 2011. [http://dx.doi.org/10.1109/TAC.2010.2088870]

[13] M.W. Brantley, L.H. Lee, C.H. Chen, and A. Chen, "Efficient simulation budget allocation with regression", *IIE Trans.,* vol. 45, no. 3, pp. 291-308, 2013. [http://dx.doi.org/10.1080/0740817X.2012.712238]

[14] C.H. Chen, J. Lin, E. Yücesan, and S.E. Chick, "Simulation budget allocation for further enhancing the efficiency of ordinal optimization", *J. Discrete Event Dyn. Syst.: Theory Appl.,* vol. 10, pp. 251-270, 2000. [http://dx.doi.org/10.1023/A:1008349927281]

[15] K. Sinha, A. Priya, and M. Khowas, "Framework for budget allocation and optimization using particle swarm optimization", *Adv. Intell. Syst. Comput.,* vol. 509, pp. 149-158, 2017. [http://dx.doi.org/10.1007/978-981-10-2525-9_15]

[16] E.P. Chew, L.H. Lee, S.Y. Teng, and C.H. Koh, "Differentiated service inventory optimization using nested partitions and MOCBA", *Comput. Oper. Res.,* vol. 36, no. 5, pp. 1703-1710, 2009. [http://dx.doi.org/10.1016/j.cor.2008.04.006]

[17] L.H. Lee, E.P. Chew, S. Teng, and D. Goldsman, "Optimal computing budget allocation for multi-objective simulation models", *Winter Simulation Conference,* 2004

[18] R.E. Bechhofer, T.J. Santner, and D.M. Goldsman, *Design and Analysis of Experiments for Statistical Selection, Screening, and Multiple Comparisons.* John Wiley & Sons: New York, 1995.

[19]   J.R. Swisher, S.H. Jacobson, and E. Yücesan, "Discrete event simulation optimization using ranking, selection, and multiple comparison procedures: A survey", *ACM Trans. Model. Comput. Simul.,* vol. 13, pp. 134-154, 2003.
[http://dx.doi.org/10.1145/858481.858484]

[20]   S.H. Kim, and B.L. Nelson, Selecting the best system: theory and methods. *In Proceedings of the Winter Simulation Conference,* S. Chick, P.J. Sánchez, D. Ferrin, D.J. Morrice, Eds., Institute of Electrical and Electronics Engineers: Piscataway, New Jersey, 2003, pp. 101-112.

[21]   Y. Rinott, "On two-stage selection procedures and related probability-inequalities", *Commun. Stat. Theor. Methods,* vol. A7, pp. 799-811, 1978.
[http://dx.doi.org/10.1080/03610927808827671]

[22]   C.H. Chen, J. Lin, E. Yücesan, and S.E. Chick, "Simulation budget allocation for further enhancing the efficiency of ordinal optimization", *J. Discr. Event Dyn. Syst.: Theor. Appl.,* vol. 10, pp. 251-270, 2000.
[http://dx.doi.org/10.1023/A:1008349927281]

[23]   N.A. Pujowidianto, L.H. Lee, C.H. Chen, and C.M. Yap, "Optimal computing budget allocation for constrained optimization", *Winter Simulation Conference,* 2009.
[http://dx.doi.org/10.1109/WSC.2009.5429660]

[24]   L.H. Lee, E.P. Chew, S. Teng, and D. Goldsman, "Optimal computing budget allocation for multi-objective simulation models", *Proceedings of the 2004 Winter Simulation Conference,* 2004, pp. 586-594

[25]   L. Davis, *Handbook of Genetic Algorithms.* Van Nostrand Reinhold: New York, United States, 1991.

[26]   H. Al-Battaineh, and S. AbouRizk, "Optimization of intermediate-level budget allocation using a genetic algorithm", *Int. J. Archit. Eng. Constr.,* vol. 2, no. 3, 2013.
[http://dx.doi.org/10.7492/IJAEC.2013.014]

[27]   R.Y. Rubinstein, and A. Shapiro, *Discrete Event Systems: Sensitivity Analysis and Stochastic Approximation using the Score Function Method.* John Wiley & Sons, 1993.

[28]   M. Clerc, and J. Kennedy, "The particle swarm: explosion, stability, and convergence in a multi-dimensional complex space", *IEEE Trans. Evol. Comput.,* vol. 6, no. 1, pp. 58-73, 2002.
[http://dx.doi.org/10.1109/4235.985692]

[29]   R. Storn, and K. Price, "Differential evolution - a simple and efficient heuristic for global optimization over continuous spaces", *J. Glob. Optim.,* vol. 11, no. 4, pp. 341-359, 1997.
[http://dx.doi.org/10.1023/A:1008202821328]

[30]   S. Zhang, P. Chen, L.H. Lee, C.E. Peng, and C.H. Chen, "Simulation optimization using the particle swarm optimization with optimal computing budget allocation", *Proceedings of the Winter Simulation Conference,* 2011
[http://dx.doi.org/10.1109/WSC.2011.6148117]

CHAPTER 3

Research Methodology

Abstract: This chapter deals with the different stochastic model which would help us to allocate the budget to a different department as well as schemes. For the allocation of the budget, a mathematical framework is developed using a combination of traditional mathematical model and evolutionary computing based model. A combination of Optimal Computing Budget Allocation (OCBA), Genetic Algorithm (GA) and Equal Allocation (EA) is considered for generating an efficient budgeting model. We have applied soft computing approach to optimize budget allocation in different schemes through which the funds are allocated proficiently.

Keywords: Equal Allocation (EA), Genetic Algorithm (GA), Growth Rate, Optimal Computing Budget Allocation (OCBA).

3.1. BUDGET ALLOCATION SCHEME/MODEL

Indian Budget/Union Budget is the annual budget of the Republic of India. Every year on the last working day of February the Finance Minister of India delivered the budget speech in the Parliament. There are fifty-three departments working independently under the Union Budget as shown below in Table **4**.

There is an unambiguous provision for budget allocation for all the department/ministries in the Indian Constitution. Our primary objective is to create a model which will work for each department for budget allocation. A mathematical model has been designed in this section, which deals with whole union budget for the Republic of India as shown in equation (9) and following equations.

As shown in Fig. (**5**), the Indian government budget is divided into several departments. For each department we have created the mathematical model for calculating the budget. Before the year 2017, Railway budget was introduced separately along with Union Budget. From 2017 onwards the railway budget is merged with the Union Budget. Here this work has been carried out before 2017, so the rail budget is shown separately in equation 9.

Keshav Sinha, Moumita Khowas & Sudip Kumar Sahana

Table 4. Different departments in the Indian parliament.

Ministry of Agriculture.	Ministry of Minority Affairs.
Department of Atomic Energy.	Ministry of New and Renewable Energy.
Ministry of Chemicals and Fertilizers.	Ministry of Overseas Indian Affairs.
Ministry of Civil Aviation.	Ministry of Panchayati Raj.
Ministry of Coal.	Ministry of Parliamentary Affairs.
Ministry of Commerce and Industry.	Ministry of Personnel, Public Grievances, and Pensions.
Ministry of Communications and Information Technology.	Ministry of Petroleum and Natural Gas.
Ministry of Consumer Affairs, Food, and Public Distribution.	Ministry of Planning.
Ministry of Corporate Affairs.	Ministry of Power.
Ministry of Culture.	The President, Parliament, Union Public Services Commission and the Secretariat of the Vice President.
Ministry of Defense.	Ministry of Road Transport and Highways.
Ministry of Development of North Eastern Region.	Ministry of Rural Development.
Ministry of Earth Science.	Ministry of Science and Technology.
Ministry of Environment and Forests.	Ministry of Shipping.
Ministry of External Affairs.	Ministry of Social Justice and Empowerment.
Ministry of Finance.	Department of Space.
Ministry of Food Processing Industries.	Ministry of Statistics and Program Implementation.
Ministry of Health and Family Welfare.	Ministry of Steel.
Ministry of Heavy Industries and Public Enterprises.	Ministry of Textiles.
Ministry of Home Affairs.	Ministry of Tourism.
Ministry of Housing and Urban Poverty Alleviation.	Ministry of Tribal Affairs.
Ministry of Human Resource Development.	Union Territories (Without Legislature).
Ministry of Information and Broadcasting.	Ministry of Urban Development.
Ministry of Labor and Employment.	Ministry of Water Resources.
Ministry of Micro, Small and Medium Enterprises.	Ministry of Women and Child Development.
Ministry of Mines.	Ministry of Youth Affairs and Sports.
Ministry of Law and Justices.	

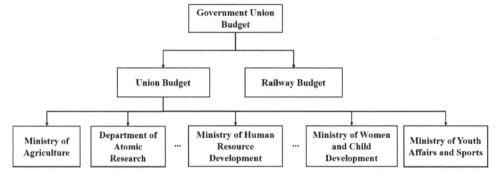

Fig. (5). Indian Budgeting Infrastructure.

Government Budget = $\{\sum_{i=1}^{53}$ Total (Expenditure on Individual Department) +

Total (Expenditure on Railway Department) $\geq$ Total Revenue$\}$ $\qquad$ **(9)**

Whereas, i = Number of Union Budget Department

Each of the departments is having some schemes for budget allocation. The funds need to be allocated for each unit one by one. We have chosen the Ministry of Human Resource & Development (MHRD) to apply our mathematical model. In the same way, the process will follow for all departments. If the model works for MHRD, it is assumed to be suited for the rest 53 departments/ministries including the Railways. The department of MHRD is divided into two sub-sections as shown in Fig. (**6**).

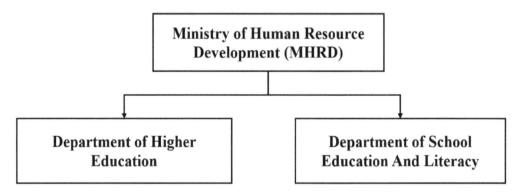

Fig. (6). MHRD Department Infrastructure.

The overall budget for MHRD department is calculated as shown in equation (10).

MHRD Budget = $\{\sum_{i=1}^{n}$ Total (Expenditure on each department of Higher Education) + $\sum_{j=1}^{n}$ Total(Expenditure on dept. of School Education and Literacy) $\geq$ Money allotted in MHRD Department$\}$ **(10)**

Whereas:

i = number of sub-department in Higher Education.

j = number of sub-department in School Education and Literacy.

n = department count.

There are two sub branches in MHRD. For the sake of simplicity, we have chosen only school education and literacy department as shown in Fig. (**7**) to make budget allocation. School education and literacy department were divided into three subgroups. Each group consists of different schemes. Each project was evaluated regarding accuracy, performance, and requirement so that we could allocate the suitable amount to these departments.

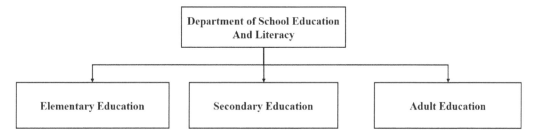

Fig. (7). School Education and Literacy Infrastructure.

To calculate the budget for school education and literacy, we use a mathematical model which is shown in equation (11).

Budget of School Education and Literacy = $[(\sum_{i=1}^{n}$ Total (Expenditure on Elementary Education) + $\sum_{j=1}^{n}$ Total (Expenditure on Secondary Education) + $\sum_{k=1}^{n}$ Total (Expenditure on Adult Education)) $\geq$ Money allocated in school Education and Literacy] **(11)**

Whereas,

i = number of sub-scheme in Elementary Education

j = number of sub-scheme in Secondary Education

k = number of sub-scheme in Adult Education

n = scheme count.

We have considered the evaluation of schemes in the secondary education department for budget allocation. For calculating the overall system's amount, the mathematical model has setup as shown in the equation (12). Fig. **(8)** will give the overall view of the secondary educational scheme.

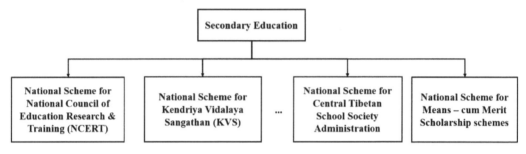

Fig. (8). Secondary Education Scheme Infrastructure.

Secondary_Education_Budget = $\{\sum_{i=1}^{n}$ Total (Expenditure on Secondary Education) ≥ Money allocated in Secondary Education$\}$ **(12)**

Whereas,

i = number of schemes.

n = number of plan count.

A small budgeting model for simulation [5] is considered for proper understanding and debugging if any error occurs. In secondary education, 15 different schemes run in parallel. For the evaluation of those plans, a survey has been consulted for the performance of each project. The various Secondary Education programs are as follows:

a. National Scheme for National Council of Education Research & Training (NCERT).
b. National Scheme for Kendriya Vidyalaya Sangathan (KVS).
c. National Scheme for Navodaya Vidyalaya Samiti (NVS).
d. National Scheme for Rashtriya Madhyamik Shiksha Abhiyan (RMSA).
e. National Scheme for setting up of 6000 model schools at the block level as a benchmark of Excellence.
f. National Scheme for Information & Communication Technology in Schools.

g. National Scheme for Inclusive Education for the Disabled at Secondary School (IEDSS).

h. National Scheme for National Institute of Open Schooling (NIOS).

i. National Scheme for Access and Equity.

j. National Scheme for Central Tibetan School Society Administration.

k. National Scheme for Vocationalisation of Education.

l. National Scheme for Incentive to Girls for Secondary Education (Success).

m. National Scheme for construction and running of Girls Hostels for students of Secondary & Higher Secondary Schools.

n. National Scheme for Appointment of Language Teacher.

o. National Scheme for Means – cum Merit Scholarship schemes.

To calculate the budget for these secondary education plans, we have taken the Growth Rate as one of the parameters which is used for allocation of the indefinite amount for the next year. The work has presented in two parts (i) Budget Optimization and (ii) Budget Allocation.

3.2. BUDGET OPTIMIZATION TECHNIQUE

After an exhaustive study of different research papers, the methodology for solving budget allocation problem has been suggested and proposed as shown in Fig. (**9**).

3.2.1. Proposed Evolutionary Computing based Framework for Budget Allocation and Optimization

The budget allocation is an essential part of an annual economic blueprint for organizations. It also specifies the resource utilization for departmental schemes. Without the proper allocation of budget, expenditure limit can exceed the revenues and result in a financial shortfall in the economy. So, to ensure proper allocation of the budget, a framework has been proposed which consists of several methods for budget allocation and the optimization [1 - 3]. The Allocation technique divided into two parts (i) Mathematical approach, and (ii) Evolutionary Computing approach. A Mathematical approach consists of several traditional methods such as growth rate, percentage growth rate and means & variance technique. While the evolutionary approach consists of biological behavior based Genetic algorithm and OCBA approach. We have used these two methods for the allocation of funds in different schemes by considering the average effect of all the results and find the nearest solution to the growth rate.

The step by step procedure for proposed Budget Allocation and Optimization strategy is discussed as follows:

1. **Step 1:** The first stage for budget allocation is initialization. The objective behind is to store the different departmental information in the form of rows and columns. Each row and column is made up of scheme name and how much fund allocated to that plan. According to Table **4**, there are 53 departments and each department has different projects. So, our model of simulation can work for each department as well as projects of each department. We need to select the department projects for budget allocation.

2. **Step 2:** After selection, we need to allocate the indefinite amount for the scheme. For that, we are following two types of budget allocation approach (i) Mathematical Finance, and (ii) Evolutionary Computing Approach. The Mathematical Finance will develop and spread the mathematical or numerical simulations without establishing a necessary link to financial theory.

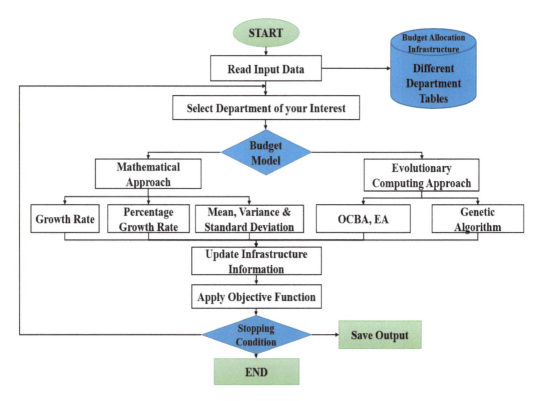

Fig. (9). Solution strategy for Budget Allocation and Optimization.

3.2.1.1. Mathematical Finance

In (1926) Ragnar Frisch, an economist developed the mathematical model in the context of economic demands and utility functions. Mathematical Finance or Quantitative Finance is a field of applied mathematics which is mostly concerned with the financial markets. Mathematical Finance (MF) will reduce and stretch the mathematical/numerical models and establish a link with the economic theory which will take a market price as an input for simulation. Mathematical finance is a heavily intersected field in computational finance and financial engineering. The primary focus is to develop the stochastic asset model for application and simulation. The Model used for quantitative analysis, and it works as a tool for implementing the model also. Our aim of this section is to allocate the budget for Indian government in a field of Secondary Education Sector by using mathematical financial models. We use these models for allocation and predicting the tentative amount of the budget for next year. The fundamental theorems (Mean and Standard Deviation, Growth Rate, and Percent Growth, *etc.*) are one of the essential budgeting techniques in mathematical finance for budget allocation.

3.2.1.1.1. Growth Rate

In macro economy, an amount recorded in discrete periods of times in quarterly or yearly. It is often useful to model the dynamic economy at a separate time. The Growth Rate calculated as an output for every year divided by the number of population in that year of any scheme.

Fig. (**10**), depicts the overall information about how the annual growth rate is calculated for any scheme. The General mathematical model for Growth Rate calculation is derived as:

Let us consider 'g' be the annual growth rate of 'Y' in any year and annual percentage change in 'Y' from last year. Therefore,

$$g_t = \hat{Y}_t \qquad\qquad (13)$$

According to annual growth rate:

$$g_t = \frac{y_t - y_{t-1}}{Y_{t-1}} \qquad\qquad (14)$$

It will define in this way that, growth rates compounded over time. Starting and at times (t=0) in equation 14, we get

$$g_1 = \frac{y_1 - y_0}{Y_0} \qquad\qquad (15)$$

Solving the equation 13 and 14 for Y_1. We get

$$Y_1 = (1+g_1). Y_0 \tag{16}$$

Similarly, for Y2, we get

$$Y_2 = (1+g_2). Y_2 => (1+g_2). (1+g_1). Y_0 \tag{17}$$

Then for any future time t' we get.

$$Y_t = [(1+g_1). (1+g_2)\dots (1+g_t)]. Y_0 \tag{18}$$

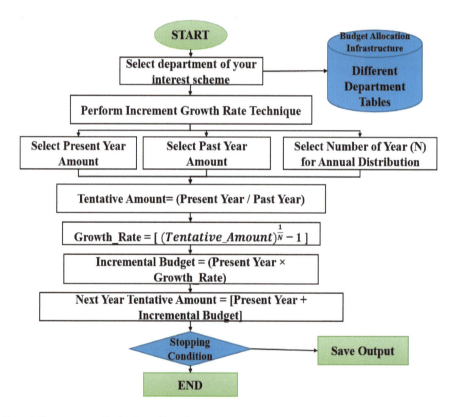

Fig. (10). Growth Rate strategy for budget allocation.

In this work, we have used the Enhanced Growth Rate formula as a parameter for predicting the indefinite amount for the next year.

The step by step implementation strategy discussed as below:

I. The first move is to select the department as per your interest. The selection process is prepared according to the list of units given at the outset of this chapter. Various agencies are having different schemes running. Based on the performance and requirement the evaluation proceeds further.

II. The next step is to apply the Enhanced Growth Rate Technique for tentative amount allocation is shown in equation (19).

$$\text{Growth} = \frac{\text{Present year} - \text{Past year}}{\text{Past Year}} \qquad (19)$$

Furthermore, solving the equation (19), we get:

$$\text{Present Year} = \text{Past Year} \times (1+\text{Growth})^n \qquad (20)$$

Therefore:

$$\text{Growth Rate (GR)} = \left[\left(\frac{\text{Present year}}{\text{Past Year}}\right)^{\frac{1}{n}} - 1\right] \qquad (21)$$

Whereas,

n = number of years for annual distribution.

Using equation (21), for finding the Incremental Budget the formulation has given as in equation (22).

$$\text{Incremental Budget} = [\text{present year} \times \text{growth rate}] \qquad (22)$$

III. For finding the next year tentative amount, the present year value is added with Incremental Budget which is given in equation (22), as shown in equation (23).

$$\text{Next year tentative amount} = [\text{Present Year} + \text{Incremental Budget}] \qquad (23)$$

IV. After the planning horizon is reached, stop the allocation process and select the new scheme for predicting.

3.2.1.1.2. Percent Growth Rate

The annual amount is increasing at every period. So, it is valuable to calculate the percentage of the amount increasing every year, which will provide the blueprint for how much increment is needed. Percentage Growth Rate is the method which is used for calculating how much cost increased annually, half yearly or quarterly. In Fig. (**11**), the working principle for calculating the percent growth rate is explained.

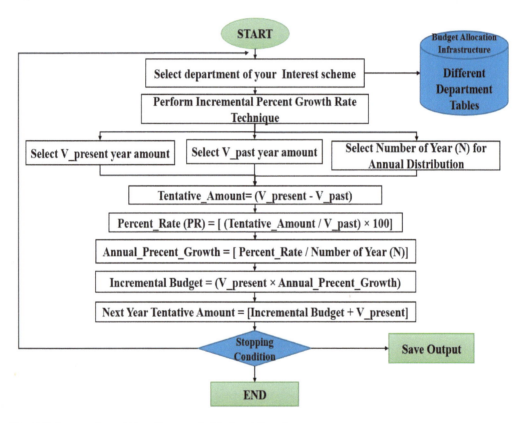

Fig. (11). Percent Growth Rate Strategy for Budget Allocation.

I. The first step is to select the department as per your interest in budget allocation.
II. The second step is to apply the incremental percent rate technique. The formula is given by equation (24).

$$PR = \frac{V_{present} - V_{past}}{V_{past}} \times 100 \qquad (24)$$

Whereas,

PR= Percent Rate.

$V_{present}$ = Present or Future Value.

V_{past} = Past or Present Value.

III. The next step is to select the $V_{present}$, V_{past}, and Number of years (n) for annual distribution.

IV. To find the tentative amount of the budget is given as equation (25).

$$Tentative\_Amount = [V_{present} - V_{past}] \qquad (25)$$

V. Using the equation (25) for calculation of Percent rate (PR), the formulation provided in equation 26.

$$PR = [Tentative\_Amount / V_{past}] \times 100 \qquad (26)$$

VI. Equation 27 gives the Annual Percent Growth.

$$Annual\_Precent\_Growth = \left[\frac{Precent\_Rate \ (PR)}{Number \ of \ Year \ (N)} \right] \qquad (27)$$

VII. For calculating increment in the next year budget, Increment Budget calculated as shown equation 28.

$$Incremental\_budget = \left[\frac{Vpresent}{Annual\_Precent\_Growth} \div 100 \right] \qquad (28)$$

VIII. The next year predictive or tentative amount calculated as Equation 29.

$$Next\_Year\_Tentative \ Amount = [Incremental\_budget + V_{present}] \qquad (29)$$

IX. After calculation when planning the horizon is reached, save the output and select the new scheme for evaluation.

3.2.1.1.3. Mean, Variance and Standard Deviation

The mean is the value that can replace every existing item in sample space, and has the best result of all. Fig. (**12**), shows the calculation technique mean and standard deviation regarding budget allocation.

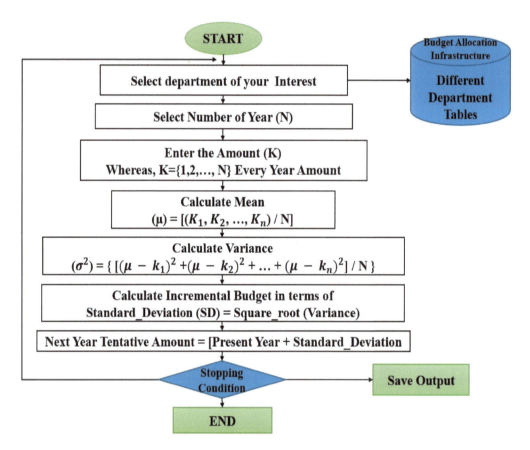

Fig. (12). Mean, Variance and Standard Deviation Technique for Budget Allocation.

I. The first step is to select the department from the budget allocation infrastructure model.

II. Next step is to choose the number of years in N.

III. The 'K' denotes the amount allocated annually. For calculation, enter the allotted amount of every year. Calculate the mean value.

$$\overline{X} = \frac{1}{N} \sum_{i=1}^{n} X \qquad (30)$$

Whereas,

$\overline{X}$ = Symbol for the sample mean.

n = Sample Size

X = Observed Valued.

IV. For calculating the mean of the budget, we use the equation (30), then

$$\overline{X} = \frac{K_1 + K_2 + K_3 + \cdots + K_n}{N} \qquad (31)$$

Whereas,

K = Year wise amount.

N = sample size.

V. For calculating the difference between the mean and actual value, the variance formula is used. Using equation (31) for the value of the mean ($\overline{X}$), calculation of variance is performed as shown in equation (32).

$$\text{Variance } (\sigma)^2 = \frac{[(\overline{X}-K_1)^2 + (\overline{X}-K_2)^2 + \cdots + (\overline{X}-K_n)^2]}{N} \qquad (32)$$

VI. The calculation of standard deviation (SD) using the equation (32) shown in equation (33).

$$\text{Standard Deviation (SD)} = \sqrt{\text{Variance}} \qquad (33)$$

VII. For prediction of the next year tentative amount by using the equation (33) the Present Year value, is shown in equation (34).

$$\text{Next Year Tentative Amount} = [\text{Present Year} + \text{Standard Deviation}] \qquad (34)$$

VIII. The last step is to save the output value and then select the new scheme for the evaluation.

3.2.1.2. Evolutionary Computing Approach

Evolutionary Programming was first announced by Lawrence J. Fogell in the US, while John Henry Holland termed his technique a Genetic Algorithm. The evolutionary computation technique is a sub field of computational intelligence. This method is theoretically fit for the intimate of experimental and inaccurate problem solver, and it is a global optimization approach with an empirical or stochastically optimal character. It is more-known from its use of a population of candidate explanations relatively than just repeating over one point in exploring space. These are frequently functional for a black box problem. Evolutionary computation uses the iterative growth in a population. This population is selected in a directed unplanned search using parallel processing to accomplish the preferred expiration genetic mechanisms of evolution often motivate such methods. In this book, we have used two evolutionary computing techniques (i) Optimal Computing Budget Allocation, and (ii) Genetic Algorithm for our simulation purposes.

3.2.1.2.1. Optimal Computing Budget Allocation (OCBA)

OCBA [4] is the evolutionary computing approach used for perceptively allocating the budget for efficient simulation and optimization time. The primary objective is to achieve the maximum replication decision quality using a fixed computing budget. A serious motive of replication optimization is computing the stochastic nature of the objective function which means that, there is a fundamental fine-tuning among assigning the computational strength on the search space for the new candidate solutions in competition with receiving more faultless approximations of the objective function on former likely explanations. The already visited points and newly generated replications examined regarding points which are a key consideration for computational efficiency. In OCBA, we decide which design need more stimulation and in what way supplementary replications can be executed. So, we conduct the simulation to obtain the preliminary solution. Fig. (**13**) shows the framework for OCBA technique. The parameters of OCBA Algorithm for selection and replication of budget are:

K = Number of Models.

T = Total Budget Simulation.

N_i^l = Budget Replication for model 'i' during 'l' number of iterations.

Δ = Budget increment after each simulation.

n_0 = Budget Initialization.

b = Best model estimation.

l = Number of iterations.

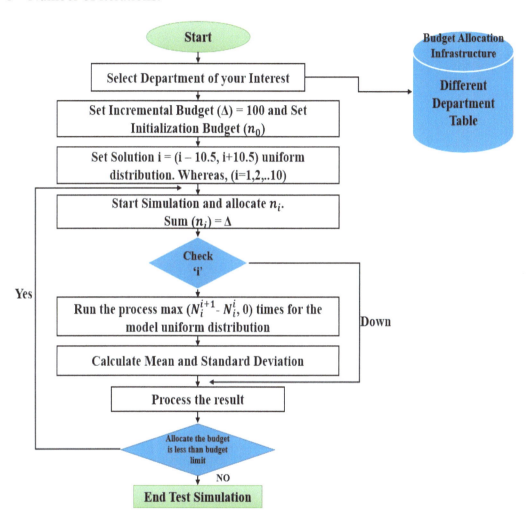

Fig. (13). Framework for Optimal Computing Budget Allocation.

The following steps describe the working principle of the OCBA technique for budget allocation.

i. The first move is to select the department from budget allocation infrastructure.

ii. For starting the simulation process first set up the incremental budget and initialization budget value.

iii. The value 'i' is uniformly distributed throughout the (i-10.5 to i+10.5) the model used for simulation.

Algorithm for OCBA

Input= K, T, Δ, n_0.

Initialize l=0, sum $(n_i) = \Delta$.

Start (run): Perform n_0 imitation reproductions

$$N_1^l = N_2^l = ... = N_K^l = n_0.$$

While

{

Simulated Budget < Total Simulation Budget

Do

Allocation

Increment the calculating budget by Δ.

Calculate a new economic budget allocation,

$N_1^{l+1}, N_2^{l+1} ... N_K^{l+1}$

For sample Mean and Standard Deviations.

Start Simulation

Find max $(N_i^{l+1} - N_1^l, 0)$

Simulate the design i,

Where i = [1, 2, 3... K]

}

End

Stop

iv. Check the result with the 'K' if yes start the simulation else stop the test simulation and check the Probability of Correct Selection (PCS).

v. The PCS lies in between the (0 to 1) if the value is near to '1' select the peak value and store the best result.

vi. Stop simulation.

3.2.1.2.2. Genetic Algorithm

Genetic Algorithms (GA) [5], is motivated by Darwin's theory of evolution. GA Algorithm begins with a set of solutions called population. The solution from one population is taken and used to form a new population. In Fig. (**14**), shows the overall framework for budget allocation.

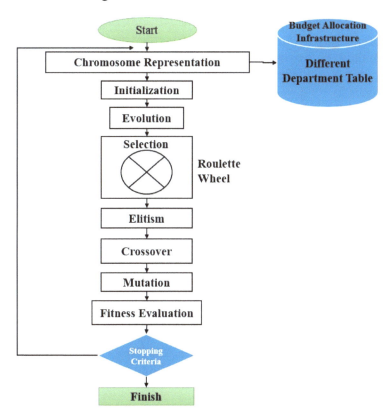

Fig. (14). Framework for Genetic Algorithm based Budget Allocation.

i. The first step is to select the value for initialization of budget allocation infrastructure. For that, a function is created for the genetic algorithm.

F (x) = {(Year 1 + Year 2 + Year 3 + Year 4 + Year 5 + Year 6)

$$F(x) = \{(\text{Year } 1 + \text{Year } 2 + \text{Year } 3 + \text{Year } 4 + \text{Year } 5 + \text{Year } 6)$$

$$\geq \text{Growth Rate}\} \tag{35}$$

There are six variables in the objective function. So, we compose the chromosome as follows:

1	2	3	4	5	6

To speed up the computation, we can restrict the value of variables up to growth rate.

ii. The second step is to select the value for initialization. Once the appropriate representation has is decided for chromosomes, it is required to generate an initial population. We define the number of chromosomes in the population as 100; then we make the random values give 1, 2, 3, 4, 5, 6 for the 100 chromosomes.

$$\sum_{i=1}^{100} Chromosome\ (i) = \text{Rand } [1, 2, 3, 4, 5, 6] \tag{36}$$

iii. The third step is an evolution where we compute the objective function value for each chromosome produced initialization item:

$$\sum_{i=1}^{100} \text{F\_Objective } [i] = \text{Abs } [(\text{Rand } (1) + \text{Rand } (2) + \dots + \text{Rand } (6))$$

$$- \text{Growth Rate}] \tag{37}$$

iv. The fourth step is selection, where the fittest chromosomes have a higher probability to be selected for the next generation. To compute fitness probability, we must compute the fitness of each chromosome. For avoiding divided by zero problems, the value of F_ Objective is added by 1.

$$\sum_{i=1}^{100} Fitness\ [i] = \frac{1}{(1+F_{Objective}[i])} \tag{38}$$

Therefore,

$$\text{Total} = \text{Fitness } [1] + \text{Fitness } [2] + \dots + \text{Fitness } [100] \tag{39}$$

Whereas,

i = 1 to 100.

The probability of each chromosome is formulated by

$$P[i] = \frac{Fitness\,[i]}{Total} \tag{40}$$

Whereas,

i = number of fitness iteration.

From the probability above to select the highest fitness for the next generation chromosome, we use a roulette wheel selection. For that, we should compute the cumulative probability values.

Cumu_Probability (1) = P (1)

Cumu_Probability (2) = P (1) + P (2)

...

Cumu_Probability (100) = P (1) + P (2) ...P (100) = 1

After calculating the aggregate probability of selection using a roulette - wheel process, generate random number 'R' in the range [0 - 1] as follows:

$$R[i] = Rand[j] \tag{41}$$

Whereas,

i =number of iterations.

j= random values.

If random number R [1] is greater than P [1] and smaller than P [2] then select Chromosome [2] as a chromosome in the new population for the next generation:

New Chromosome [1] = Chromosome [2]

New Chromosome [2] = Chromosome [3]

...

New Chromosome [100] = Chromosome [96]

v. The next step is elitism. The concept behind this to keep the best solution unharmed during the reproduction. The top 5-10% solution is copied intact from the current generation to the next generation without any crossover and mutation. So, in this research, we take top 5% of the chromosome production for relocation of new generation process.

vi. While Crossover, the chromosome is selected for producing the offspring. The probability of selecting the crossover is lying in between 0.0 to 1.0. Where 1.0 indicates that all the selected chromosomes used for the reproduction that means there are no survivors. We use uniform crossover mechanism in which the random bits are copied from the first parent or the second parent. For the better result of crossover, we select the crossover probability 0.65 to 0.85. If we use only crossover operator for offspring, then some problems may arise which is illustrated in the example. For example, in the population the chromosomes have a '0' in the position then all future offspring will have a '0' at position too. To overcome this type of undesirable situation a mutation is used.

Parent A	Parent B	Offspring
11111111	00000000	10100111

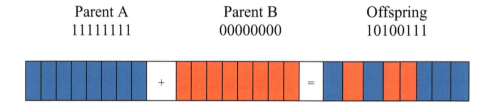

Randomly select a position in the parent chromosome, then exchange sub-chromosomes. Parent chromosome, which will mate, is randomly selected, and the number of mate chromosomes are controlled using crossover rate (ρc) parameter. Next generations generate new generations of solutions. Each subsequent generation obtains the partial solution. Eventually, the population produces the offspring which is different from the previous generations. The pseudo code presentation of crossover process for selection of chromosome is as follows:

Pseudo code for the Crossover Process

Begin k← 0;

While (k<population)

do

R[k] ← random (0-1);

If (R[k] < ρc)

Select Chromosome [k] as a parent;

End;

k = k + 1;

End;

End;

Chromosome 'k' is selected as a parent if R [k] < ρc. Suppose that we set the crossover rate is 35%, then Chromosome number 'k' is selected for crossover, if the randomly generated value for Chromosome 'k' below 0.35. The process is as follows:

First, we generate a random number R as the number of population.

$$R\ [k] = Rand\ [l] \tag{42}$$

Whereas,

k =number of iterations.

l = random values.

For random number R above, we select the parents for crossover.

Chromosome [1] >< Chromosome [4]

...

Chromosome [100] >< Chromosome [89]

After chromosome selection, the next process is determining the position of the crossover point. For point selection, a random number is generating between 1 to length of chromosome. In this case, generated random numbers should be between 1 and 3.

After we get the crossover point, parents chromosome will cut at the crossover point, and the genes will interchange the position. For example, we generated '3' random numbers, and we get:

C [1] = 1

C [2] = 1

C [3] = 2

Then for the first, second and third crossover, the parents' genes will be cut in gene number 1, gene number 1 and gene number 3 respectively.

vii. In mutation, the random alteration of the genes occurs. It means '0' becomes '1' and *vice versa*. Typically, this has not frequently occurred, so mutation is the order of one bit changed in a thousand tests. Where each bit in population is checked for possible mutation by generating a random number between 0.0 and 1.0 and if this quantity is less than or equal to the given mutation probability value then the bit value is changed. For selecting the value of the mutation rate, it is accomplished by selecting the proper balance between exploration and exploitation of the algorithm. In other words, if the high mutation rate shrinks, the search ability of GA is just simple dummy random walk, while the small mutation rate may result in premature convergence means falling to local optima in its place of the global optimum. So, selecting the mutation probability should be nearly 0.015 to 0.02.

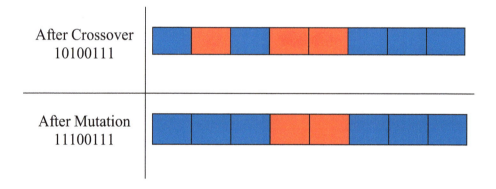

The mutation rate parameter determines the number of chromosomes that mutations have in a population by replacing the gene at random position with a new value of mutation is determined. The process is as follows:

First, we must calculate the total length of gene in the population. In this case, the entire duration of gene is:

Total_gen = num_of_gen_in_Chromosome * number of population   **(43)**

A mutation process initiated by generating a random integer between 1 and total_gen (1 to 24). If the generated random number is smaller than the mutation rate (ρm) variance, then it marks the position of gene in chromosomes. Suppose we define ρm 10%, and it's expected that 10% (0.1) of total_gen in the population is mutated. After finishing mutation process, we have one iteration or one generation of the genetic algorithm.

viii. The next step is to setup the Fitness function. For fitness evaluation, we use Mean Squared Accuracy and Sum Squared Accuracy formula for evaluation.

$$\widehat{X} = \frac{1}{n} \sum_{i=1}^{n} X_i \qquad (44)$$

$$SSA = \sum_{i=1}^{n} (\widehat{X} - X_i)^2 \qquad (45)$$

$$MSA = \frac{SSA}{n} \qquad (46)$$

Whereas,

X= number of population.

$\widehat{X}$ = mean value.

n = number of items in sample space.

In equation 44, we find the mean of the solution for getting the accuracy of the population. In equation 45, the average value is getting subtracted from each and individual value within the sample space. In equation 46, the SSA is divided by a sample space so that we can get the mean squared accuracy.

ix. We can now evaluate the objective function after one generation. For the evaluation of new Chromosome, we observe that the objective function is decreasing, this means that we have better Chromosome or solution compared with a previous Chromosome generation.

These new Chromosomes will undergo the same process as the previous generation of Chromosomes such as evaluation, selection, crossover, and mutation and at the end, it produces a new generation of Chromosome for the next iteration. This process repeated until a predetermined number of generations is not achieved.

x. At last, save the output and update the infrastructure and stop the test simulation.

3.3. BUDGET ALLOCATION TECHNIQUE

All the simulations run for finding the tentative amount of budget allocation. Among these simulation results (Growth rate, percent growth rate, mean and standard deviation, OCBA and GA), we select the two by averaging the value of (OCBA, GA, and EA), the nearest value to Growth Rate is taken for budget allocation. The allocation is done by next four uncertain equations, which is given below. Let X_1, X_2, and X_3 be the parameters which define the corresponding budget line equation. The budget line equation used for maximization and minimization of the budget. For allocation of budget in different schemes are in following ways:

An allocation of 50% of amount using Ranking & Selection [6, 7] based Equal Allocation shown in Equation 47.

$$X_1 = S_n^{EA} = \frac{M_1}{n} \tag{47}$$

Whereas,

$$S_n^{EA} = S_1^{EA} + S_2^{EA} + \ldots + S_{n-1}^{EA}$$

Allocates 30% of amount using the prioritization technique which shown in Equation 48.

$$X_2 = M_2 \sum_{i=1}^{n} S_i^{EA} \leq M_1 \tag{48}$$

An allocation of 20% of the amount according to the necessity of the department shown in Equation 49.

$$X_3 = M_3 \sum_{j=1}^{n} S_j^{EA} \leq M_1 \tag{49}$$

The rest of the allocated amount awarded by Ranking & Selection which shown in Equation 50.

$$X_4 = S_n^{EA} = M_4 \tag{50}$$

Therefore, the **Overall Secondary Education Budget** is driven as:

$$\text{Secondary Education Budget} = \{X_1 + X_2 + X_3 + X_4 \le M\} \tag{51}$$

Whereas,

X_1, X_2, X_3, and X_4 are Budget Line Equation.

S_1, S_2 ... Sn = Number of Different Scheme for Budget Allocation.

n = Number of Different Schemes.

M = Total Tentative Fund Allocated for the Department.

M_1 (Half of the Fund) $= \dfrac{M}{2}$.

$M_2 = \dfrac{M_1}{n} \times \dfrac{20}{100}$ (Total Fund Allocated - Half of the Fund).

$M_3 = \{M_2 - \dfrac{M_1}{n} \times \dfrac{30}{100} \}$

$M_4 = \dfrac{M1 - (M2 + M3)}{n}$

By using Budget Optimization and Allocation Technique, we can update the infrastructure for the Budget Allocation.

Step 4: Objective function has applied for budget allocation in different schemes. The motive of the objective function is to evaluate the result and predict whether the amount allocated to projects are efficient and better or not.

Step 5: Check whether the fund is assigned to every department or not in a proficient manner. If the resource is allocated efficiently or in optimum way, then stopping criteria is achieved else we select the department for test simulation again.

Step 6: Save the output and move for the next scheme for evaluation.

CONCLUDING REMARKS

This section consists of various methods for allocation and optimization used for preparing the budget allocation model. The distribution proceeds in two different ways. First, the mathematical finance where it calculates the indefinite amount for budget and second, where the Allocation prepared according to the evolutionary computing technique. After optimization, the infinite amount allocated in the different scheme by using an innovative way. In this allocation, each department can get the amount according to its demand and effectiveness. And at last the rest unallocated amount is distributed in each scheme equally.

CONSENT FOR PUBLICATION

Not applicable.

CONFLICT OF INTEREST

This presentation certifies that authors have no affiliations with or involvement in any organization or entity with any financial interest (such as honoraria, educational grants, participation in speakers' bureaus, membership, employment, consultancies, stock ownership, or other equity interest; and expert testimony or patent-licensing arrangements), or Non-financial interest (such as personal or professional relationships, affiliations, knowledge or beliefs) in the subject matter or materials discussed in this manuscript.

ACKNOWLEDGEMENTS

For the preparation of this chapter, we would like to thank economist Dr. Soumonanda Dinda, Dept. of Economics, the University of Burdwan for his great support.

Finally, we like to acknowledge and thankful to the publisher of this book "Bentham Publisher" for its wide circulation and make a provision to reach this article to some readers.

REFERENCES

[1] J. Pichitlamken, and B.L. Nelson, "Selection-of-the-best procedure for optimization *via* simulation", *Winter Simulation Conference,* 2001

[2] S. Srivastava, S.K. Sahana, D. Pant, and P.K. Mahanti, "Hybrid microscopic discrete evolutionary model for traffic signal optimization", *J. Next Gen. Inf. Tech.,* vol. 6, no. 2, pp. 1-6, 2015. [JNIT].

[3] K. Sinha, A. Priya, and M. Khowas, "Framework for budget allocation and optimization using particle swarm optimization", *Adv. Intel. Syst. Comput.,* vol. 509, pp. 149-158, 2017.
[http://dx.doi.org/10.1007/978-981-10-2525-9_15]

[4] N.A. Pujowidianto, L.H. Lee, C.H. Chen, and C.M. Yap, "Optimal computing budget allocation for

constrained optimization", *Winter Simulation Conference,* 2009
[http://dx.doi.org/10.1109/WSC.2009.5429660]

[5]　　H. Al-Battaineh, and S. AbouRizk, "Optimization of intermediate-level budget allocation using a genetic algorithm", *Int. J. Arch. Eng. Constr.,* vol. 2, no. 3, 2013.
[http://dx.doi.org/10.7492/IJAEC.2013.014]

[6]　　J.D. Gibbons, I. Olkin, and M. Sobel, "An introduction to ranking and selection", *Am. Stat.,* vol. 33, no. 4, 1979.

[7]　　J.R. Swisher, S.H. Jacobson, and E. Yücesan, "Discrete event simulation optimization using ranking, selection, and multiple comparison procedures: A survey", *ACM Trans. Model. Comput. Simul.,* vol. 13, pp. 134-154, 2003.
[http://dx.doi.org/10.1145/858481.858484]

CHAPTER 4

Result and Discussion

Abstract: This chapter deals with the result section of budget allocation and optimization of the Secondary Education department of the Republic of India which has many schemes. Plot wise prediction is carried out and compared with the available reports to analyze the accuracy and effectiveness. The output shows that, the developed model has a great potential to allocate and optimize funds and also provides a high agreement for validation of the said mathematical model for budget allocation.

Keywords: Equal Allocation (EA), Genetic Algorithm (GA), Growth Rate, Optimal Computing Budget Allocation (OCBA).

Simulation work has been performed using Eclipse Indigo programming paradigm version 12.1 on Windows 8.1 platform, having a hardware specification: Processor Intel core i5, CPU frequency 1.70GHz Single Core Processor, 4GB RAM on x64-bit operating system. In Table **5**, year wise allocated amount has been shown for different schemes in secondary education.

Table 5. The year wise amount allocated in Secondary Education Schemes.

SCHEME	2009	2010	2011	2012	2013	2014	2015
National Council of Education Research and Training (NCERT)	137.41	147.3	170	227.7	243.3	259.72	225
Kendriya Vidyalaya Sangathan (KVS)	2112.8	2002	2235	2436.24	2599.24	3290.8	3278.47
Navodaya Vidyalaya Samiti (NVS)	1641.29	1755.4	1608.8	1701.05	1748.29	2038.4	2061
Rashtriya Madhyamik Shiksha Abhiyan (RMSA)		1700	2423.9	3124	3983	5000	3565	1353.98
Scheme for setting up of 6000 model school at block level	350	425	1200	1080	1000	1200	1
Information and communication Technology in schools	300	400	500	350	350	0	0
Integrated Education for disabled children	0	0	0	0	0	0	0
Inclusive education for the disabled at secondary school (IEDSS)	70	70	100	70	50	0	0
National Institute of open schooling	15	15	15	0.1	0.1	0	0

(Table 5) contd.....

SCHEME	2009	2010	2011	2012	2013	2014	2015
Access and Equity	0.01	0.5	0.1	0.1	0	0	1
Central Tibetan schools society Administration	38	39.82	45	49	52.14	55.85	50
Vocationalisation of Education	37	25	25	100	80.1	0	0
Scheme for universal access and quality at the secondary stage SUCCESS	0	45	45	0	0	0	0
National Scheme For Incentive To Girls For Secondary Education SUCCESS	50	95	230	100	100	0	0
National Merit Scholarship Scheme	0	0	0	0	0	0	0
New Model School	0	0	0	0	0	0	0
Upgrading 2000 KGBVs residential schools, hostel/girls hostel	0	0	0	0	0	0	0
Scheme for construction and running of girls hostels	60	10	25	450	450	0	0
Appointment of language teacher	16	15	5	6	5.8	0	0
National means-cum merit scholarship for class 9 to 12	75	90.5	60	70	70	0	0
Other programs	3.6	4.08	4	3.8	2.7	2.7	2.7
Total	6606.11	7563.5	9391.9	10626.99	11751.67	10412.47	6973.15

The experimental results for budget allocation have been drawn according to the Growth Rate, Percent Growth Rate, and Mean & Standard Deviation, as a parameter for Optimal Computing Budget Allocation [1], EA and Genetic Algorithm [2].

4.1. TEST CASE 1: GROWTH RATE CALCULATION

Growth Rate is referred to the percentage change in amount, within a period in a particular context. For fund regulation, the growth rates typically represent the compounded annual rate of growth in revenues, earnings, dividends and even macro concepts such as GDP of the economy. The Growth Rate data set for the Secondary Education is cited in Table **6**.

Table 6. Secondary Education Amount Allocation.

Year	Amount	Growth Rate %
2009	6606.11	-
2010	7563.50	14.49
2011	9391.90	24.17

(Table 6) contd.....

Year	Amount	Growth Rate %
2012	10626.99	13.15
2013	11751.67	10.58
2014	10412.47	11.39
2015	6973.15	-33.03
2016	7036.27	0.9052

Table **6** shows the year-wise allocated amount for the Secondary Education. Applying the mathematical model of growth rate for the calculation of the tentative amount of the next year. The parameters are: present year, last year and the number of annual years. In Fig. (**15**), the graphical representation of growth rate shows the predicted Growth Rate of Next Year. Even if the year 2009 had taken a base year, then we find that the allocated amount in the year 2009 was Rs. 6606.11 Crores. The hike in Growth rate was up to 14.49% in year 2010. It got the maximum hike in growth rate in the year 2011. In the same year 2011, the budget allocation for the Secondary Education was Rs. 9391.90 Crores and the slope continued till the year 2015, when the amount allocated to Secondary school was Rs. 6973.15 Crores, having a growth rate (%) -33.03. In the year 2016, it is predicted that if the rate of increase is 0.9052%, then, the amount allocation on secondary education will be Rs. 7036.27 Crores. It will be much satisfactory and near to the Government Budget as Predicted.

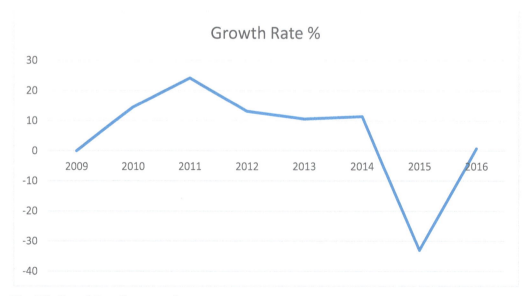

Fig. (15). Growth Rate Representation.

In Figs. (**15** and **16**), the amount of budget allocation is shown, which explicitly indicates that, in the year 2011, the amount was allocated maximum as predicted in the year 2016. This was more than the year 2015, and much probably lie in between 7000 to 9000.

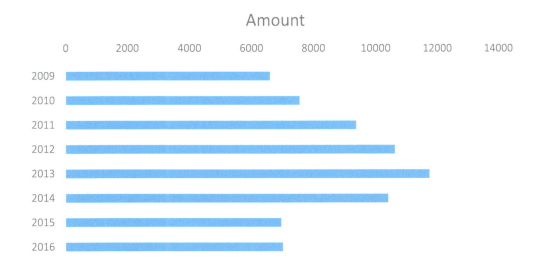

Fig. (16). Predicted Amount Allocation.

4.2. TEST CASE 2: PERCENT GROWTH RATE

The Percent Growth Rate (%) data set is cited in Table **7**. In the table given below, the percentage growth rate (%) was maximum during the year 2011 and minimum during the year 2015. We find that percentage growth rate varies ultimately when the percentage growth rate predicts 5.55% against predicted amount budget allocation of Rs. 7037.72 Crores in the year 2016.

Table 7. Percent Growth Rate for Secondary Education.

Year	Amount	Percent Growth Rate %
2009	6606.11	-
2010	7563.50	14.49
2011	9391.90	24.17
2012	10626.99	13.15
2013	11751.67	10.58
2014	10412.47	-11.39
2015	6973.15	-33.03

(Table 7) contd.....

Year	Amount	Percent Growth Rate %
2016	7037.72	5.55

For calculating the indefinite amount using percent growth rate mathematical model, the parameters used for the calculation are V_present, V_past, and a number of annual years. Fig. (**17**) presents the percent growth rate curve in between the year 2009 and year 2015. The curve hikes in the year 2011 up to the maximum level and it comes to the point where the percent growth curve denominates at the juncture of (-33.03%) during the year 2015. After prediction, percentage growth rate is calculated 5.55% during the year 2016 against budget allocation Rs. 7037.72 Crores. This prediction depends on the government allocation of the amount and prediction of the growth rate. Our prediction matches the state allocation and the percentage growth rate, in the year 2016 and this gives a consolidated enunciation of the budget allocation and its result. If any whacking and upheavals do not influence the bazaar and resultant of implementing data the distribution of currencies gives favorable results in the form of percentage growth rate. The infrastructure of education works to mobilize the entire working and functional attitude of the structure.

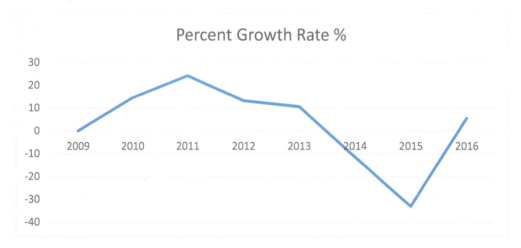

Fig. (17). Percentage Growth Rate Representation.

The consequences of any program affect the nature of government implementation of rules as we find after viewing (Fig. **17**). Fig. (**18**) presents a bar graph in which we see that the ground year for allocation of the amount was taken in the year 2009 in which price Rs. 6606.11 Crores forms skyscrapers up to the year 2014 having an increased growth of the sum. During the year 2015, it decreased and reached Rs. 6973.15 Crores. Much probably assumption is that during the year 2016 the amount of the budget will be Rs. 7037.12 Crores and it is apparently depicted in the given bar graph.

Fig. (18). Percent Rate Representation for Secondary Education.

4.3. TEST CASE 3: MEAN AND STANDARD DEVIATION TECHNIQUE

Table **8** shows the budget allocation and percentage growth rate depicted under the method of mean and standard deviation technique. In the year 2009, the amount allocated was Rs. 6606.11 Crores. It was increased during the year 2010 by Rs. 7563.50 Crores. The deviation experienced was Rs. 957.39 Crores. In the year 2011, the allocated amount was Rs. 9391.90 Crores which shows the difference of Rs. 1828.40 Crores. In the year 2012, the allocated amount was Rs. 9391.90 Crores which demonstrates the difference of Rs. 1235.09 Crores. During the year 2013, the allocated amount was Rs. 11751.67 Crores against the difference of Rs. 1124.68 Crores. In the year 2014, variation was Rs. -1339.20 Crores against the allocated amount of Rs. 10421.47 crores with a deficit. During the year 2015, the difference was Rs. -3439.32 Crores against the allocated amount of Rs. 6973.15 Crores. It is predicted that if the allocated amount will be Rs. 8834.588 Crores, the deviation will be Rs. 1861.438 Crores.

Table 8. Mean and Standard Deviation Technique.

Year	Amount	Deviation
2009	6606.11	-
2010	7563.50	957.39
2011	9391.90	1828.4

(Table 8) contd.....

Year	Amount	Deviation
2012	10626.99	1235.09
2013	11751.67	1124.68
2014	10412.47	-1339.2
2015	6973.15	-3439.32
2016	8834.588	1861.438

Table **5**, Year-wise tentative amount is calculated using mean and standard deviation which is cited in Table **5**. Using graphical representation, we show the hike in the next year. During the year 2011, we see a hike of Rs. 1828.4 Crores over the year 2010. Fig. (**19**) shows that during the year 2012 the standard deviation was Rs. 1235.09 Crores against the allocated amount of Rs. 10626.99 Crores. This hike WAS reasonably experienced continuously up to the year 2014, but a sudden down fall was seen during the year 2015.The allocated amount in the year 2015 was Rs. 6973.15 Crores with a deficit of Rs. -3439.32. If government allocates Rs. 8834.588 Crores, then the hike may be predicted as Rs. 1861.438 Crores in the year 2016.

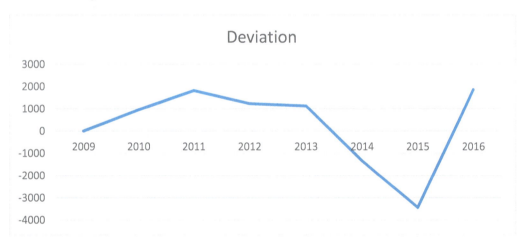

Fig. (19). Amount Deviation Representation.

Figs. (**19** and **20**) show bar graph representation of the mean and standard deviation of allocation of the fund in the secondary education system. It was observed that the budget allocation was comparatively less during the year 2009, 2010, and 2015, whereas, the assignment of the amount was more during the year 2011 and 2012, and more distribution of price during the year 2013. We also observe that in the year 2014 the result was realized in hiked condition while budget allocation was maximum during the preceding year. We predict that the amount allocated will be Rs. 8834.58 Crores, which matches the government allocation and prediction of growth during the year 2016.

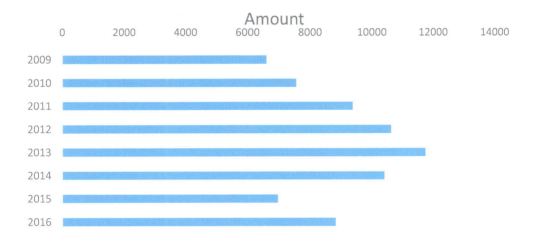

Fig. (20). Tentative Amount representation using Mean and Standard Deviation.

4.4. OPTIMIZATION TECHNIQUE 1: OCBA TECHNIQUE

For OCBA, the initial setup for budget allocation is as follows:

'K' represents the model, 'T' represents the total number of budget simulation, 'Δ' represents budget increment after each simulation, and 'n_0' is used for budget initialization. For different schemes, we change the budget allocation parameters. The selection was made according to the PCS having the maximum probability.

In Fig. (**21**), the graph represents the number of simulations in x-axis and the probability of correct selection P (CS) in y-axis. The probability of correct selection represented nearer to the '1' where the highest peak was experienced. The amount was found to be Rs. 8912 Crores which is predicted for the year 2016 budget allocation and comes out approximately as allotted by the government.

4.5. OPTIMIZATION TECHNIQUE 2: EA TECHNIQUE

Fig. (**22**) represents the EA method graph. For EA the initial setups for budget allocation is assumed such as 'K' for Number of Models, 'T' for the total number of budget simulation and 'Δ' for Budget increment after each simulation, and 'n_0' for Budget Initialization. The selection was prepared according to the maximum PCS probability. The highest peak considered at the point of budget allocation was Rs. 8911 Crores.

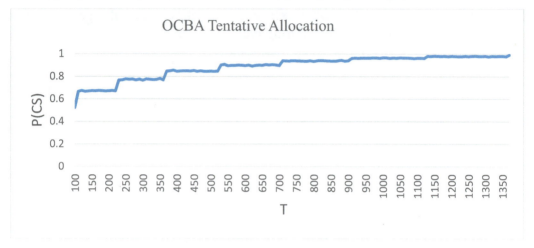

Fig. (21). OCBA Tentative Allocation of Amount having the highest PCS.

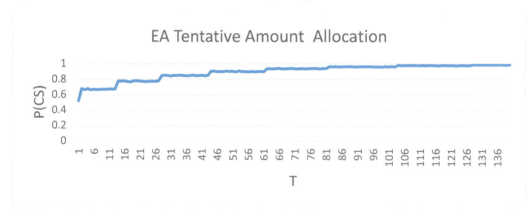

Fig. (22). EA Allocation of Tentative Amount having the highest PCS.

In OCBA Technique, where we find that the amount of budget allocation is Rs. 8912 Crores which shows that some simulations in OCBA Technique give less results than EA Technique. We observed that OCBA technique has a better result and has less number of simulations than EA when running under the same consequence.

4.6. OPTIMIZATION TECHNIQUE 3: GA OPTIMIZATION

For GA, the initial parameter is setup for Budget Allocation such as uniform rate, mutation rate, tournament size, elitism, population size. For each scheme, we change the settings so that it can give the result as per our utility. The initial parameters of the GA are uniform rate=0.5, the mutation rate=0.02, tournament size=5, and elitism = true.

In Fig. (**23**) X-axis represents the fitness value and Y-axis represents the number of generations. The primary fitness value is 5200 which is graduating after 6200. When the program runs and reaches on 9800 generation, the best fitness value is found. After this point, our objective function is satisfied. After 6200 generations, fitness value seems to be good, and the predicted value is reached near about the government expenditure. At the beginning, the fitness value was not significantly modified but after 5500 there was a hike seen in the fitness value which continuously upgraded to the zenith. The nadir point is at 0 on the X-axis which gets the apex point after 6200 at X-axis and 9800 generations.

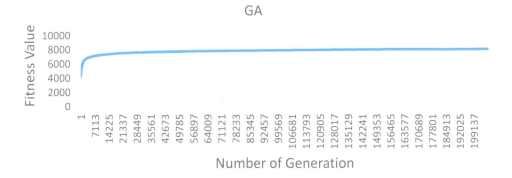

Fig. (23). Genetic Algorithm optimization for Budget Allocation.

4.7. BUDGET ALLOCATION TECHNIQUE

Table **9** shows the predicted amount using six different budget allocation methods implemented so far. Growth rate, Percentage growth rate, OCBA, EA, and GA have a comparatively approximately similar effect when these run in the same environment on the system. So, among the budget allocation techniques OCBA, EA, and GA are taken as a final method for deriving the resultant of the predicted amount.

According to the given test case results, we set the optimal parameters of OCBA, EA, and GA for selecting the indefinite amount. Out of three, the two techniques are taken for budget allocation by averaging their results which are near to the growth rate. The optimized budget for different schemes is allocated using ranking and selection process [3] in the scale of 1 to 9.

The highest ranking of the scheme is setup according to the performance of the scheme and the future aspects of that plan. According to Table **9**, the lifespan of some projects is expired. So, we do the ranking process according to the growth rate for each scheme.

Table **10** represents the allocated amount for different schemes of the secondary education system from year 2009 to 2015. The schemes like KVS, NVS, and RMSA have more allocated budget, while other schemes like NCERT and Central Tibetan School Society Administration have been given comparatively less amount for the improvement. Several older schemes have been closed for not experiencing steady and reasonable progress and growth. So the government had decided to shut down those schemes. Evaluation process was followed on different Schemes for Budget Allocation using Growth Rate technique. The amount was allocated every year for the improvement of the project. The growth rate parameter is used for allocation of budget for tentative New Year. Through the graph it is depicted that the number of schemes run under secondary education. The plans with unsatisfactory results are exempted, and the satisfactory plans are considered for further extension.

Table 9. Comparison of different techniques for tentative amount allocation.

Technique	Predicted Amount	Tentative Amount
Growth Rate	7036.27 Crores	Rs. 8774.33 Crores
Percentage Growth Rate	7037.72 Crores	
Mean and Standard Deviation	8834.588 Crores	
Optimal Computing Budget Allocation (OCBA)	8912 Crores	
Equal Allocation (EA)	8911 Crores	
Genetic Algorithm (GA)	8500 Crores	

Table 10. Year wise budget allocation in different schemas.

SCHEME	2009	2010	2011	2012	2013	2014	2015
National Council Of Educational Research And Training (NCERT)	137.41	147.3	170	227.7	243.3	259.72	225
Kendriya Vidyalaya Sangathan (KVS)	2112.8	2002	2235	2436.24	2599.24	3290.8	3278.47
Navodaya Vidyalaya Samiti (NVS)	1641.29	1755.4	1608.8	1701.05	1748.29	2038.4	2061
Rashtriya Madhyamik Shiksha Abhiyan (RMSA)	1353.98	1700	2423.9	3124	3983	5000	3565
Scheme for setting up of 6000 model school at block level	350	425	1200	1080	1000	1200	1
Information and communication Technology in schools	300	400	500	350	350	0	0
Integrated Education for disabled children	0	0	0	0	0	0	0
Inclusive education for the disabled at secondary school (IEDSS)	70	70	100	70	50	0	0

(Table 10) contd.....

SCHEME	2009	2010	2011	2012	2013	2014	2015
National Institute of open schooling	15	15	15	0.1	0.1	0	0
Access and Equity	0.01	0.5	0.1	0.1	0	0	1
Central Tibetan Schools Society Administration	38	39.82	45	49	52.14	55.85	50
Vocationalisation of Education	37	25	25	100	80.1	0	0
Scheme for universal access and quality at the secondary stage SUCCESS	0	45	45	0	0	0	0
National scheme for incentive to girls for secondary education SUCCESS	50	95	230	100	100	0	0
National Merit Scholarship Scheme	0	0	0	0	0	0	0
New Model School	0	0	0	0	0	0	0
Upgrading 2000 KGBVs residential schools, hostel/girls hostel	0	0	0	0	0	0	0

4.7.1. Scheme 1: National Council of Education Research and Training (NCERT)

Table **11** given below enunciates the amount allocation and percentage growth rate for the year 2009 to 2015. During the year 2009, the allocated amount was Rs. 137.41 Crores in NCERT which is taken as a base year. The growth rate of 7.197 percentage was depicted in the year 2010 against the amount of Rs. 147.3 Crores. It is increasingly reaching at the level of Rs. 259.72 Crores having a growth rate percentage of 5.926. But in between the year 2015, the amount was decreased to Rs. 225 Crores. Unfortunately, growth rate percentage is denominated and reached to (-12.695%). To make the profitable and progressive result in growth rate, it will have to allocate more amount to achieve more percentage growth rate. We have predicted the amount of Rs. 241.4223 Crores for the year 2016. The predicted amount shows a percentage growth rate of 7.29% which seems reasonable and near about the actual allocated amount by the government.

Table 11. Amount Allocation in NCERT Scheme.

YEAR	AMOUNT	Growth rate (%)
2009	137.41	-
2010	147.3	7.197
2011	170	15.41
2012	227.7	33.94
2013	243.3	6.85

(Table 11) contd.....

YEAR	AMOUNT	Growth rate (%)
2014	259.72	5.926
2015	225	-12.695
2016	241.4223	7.29

In NCERT scheme, Fig. (**24**) shows the graphical representation of Table **11**, in which we have experienced the growth rate percentage of the allocated amount for the year 2009 to the year 2016. After a deficit of (-12.695%), the growth rate was predicted to be 7.29% against the amount of Rs. 241.4223 Crores which gives a sudden hike in the graph as shown below.

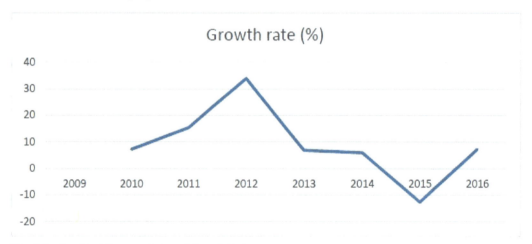

Fig. (24). Graphical Representation of Growth Rate.

Fig. (**25**) shows the bar graph representation of the allocated amount during the year 2009 to the year 2016.

The beginning of the allocation has reactions with upgrading steps reaching the maximum during the year 2014. Then, it got a jerk of the deficit during the year 2015, so the predicted amount during the year 2016 was kept a bit higher than the year 2015 (Rs. 241.4223 Crores) and so a definite hike in the bar graph is experienced as shown below.

Fig. (**26**) represents the soft computing based OCBA technique for secondary education. In x-axis, the number of generation is shown and, in y-axis, Probability of Correct Selection is shown. While simulation, we get the highest peak in the 1130 Generation. After this point, the probability reaches 1, therefore it will not be considered for our allocation.

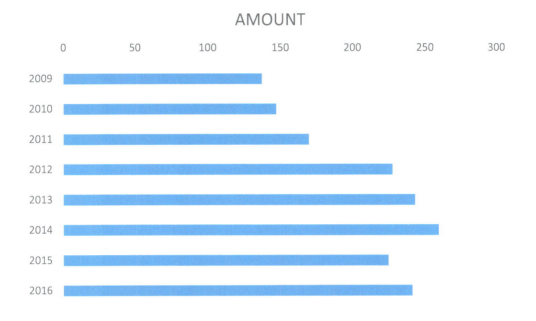

Fig. (25). NCERT Year Wise Budget Allocation.

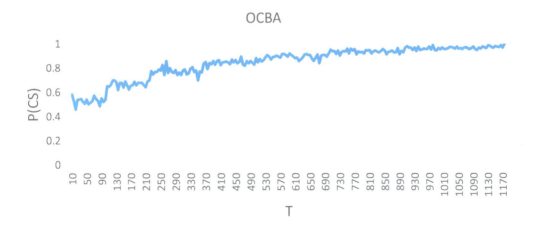

Fig. (26). OCBA Simulation Result for Tentative Amount.

Fig. (**27**) shown below represents the soft computing based EA Technique. It is observed that there are a lot of upheavals which reach a constant level after getting a hike at a 2120 generation and the probability reaches '1'.

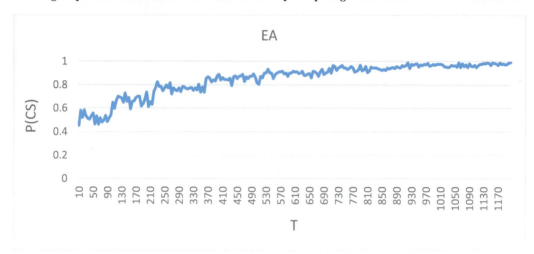

Fig. (27). EA Simulation Result for Tentative Amount.

The NCERT scheme has fewer increments for the year 2015-2016. The ranking for that plan was made according to priority and urgency of the fund. According to the growth rate, the ranking was done to get the indefinite amount for the next year for budget allocation which is shown in Table **12** given below.

Table 12. Average Amount Allocation in the NCERT Scheme.

Technique	Predicted Amount	Final Average Amount Allocation
Growth Rate	241.4233 Crores	Rs. 247 Crores
OCBA	249 Crores	
EA	247 Crores	
GA	245 Crores	

4.7.2. Scheme 2: Kendriya Vidyalaya Sangathan (KVS)

Table **13**, for Kendriya Vidyalaya Sangathan (KVS) (scheme 2) the allocated amount was Rs. 2112.80 Crores in the year 2009 and during the year 2010 growth rate percentage was obtained -5.24% against Rs. 2002 Crores. After that in the year 2011, fund allocation was increased and reached at the level of Rs. 2235 Crores which gave the growth rate percentage of 11.63%. In the year 2012, we find that budget allocation was Rs. 2436.24 Crores which gave growth rate of 9%. This increment in growth rate reaches the height of 26.6062% against the budget allocation of amount Rs. 3290.80 Crores. Again, a deficit was experienced in the growth rate percentage (-0.37%) against the allocated amount of Rs. 3278.47 Crores. To make a profitable and progressive budget, the prediction of price allocation was taken Rs. 5087.26 showing a growth rate percentage of 55.17%, which was found near about the growth of the government expenditure.

Table 13. Tentative Amount Allocation Using Growth Rate.

YEAR	AMOUNT	Growth rate (%)
2009	2112.8	
2010	2002	-5.24
2011	2235	11.63
2012	2436.24	9.00
2013	2599.24	6.69
2014	3290.8	26.6062
2015	3278.47	-0.37
2016	5087.26	55.17

In Fig. (**28**) and Table **13**, the graphical expression of budget allocation and its percentage growth are shown, respectively. Here, we find that two deficit points are obtained in the graph, in the year 2010 and year 2015. In the beginning, the government was lenient in allocating the fund in the budget and at the later stage, the helter-skelter inconsistent profitable result was seen. But the diving effect of growth rate was seen in the year 2015 and make the favorable result was observed in the year 2016. The amount was increased, and so the rate was also found to be growing during 2016.

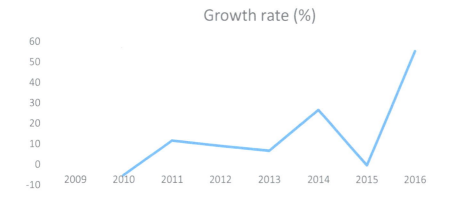

Fig. (28). Graphical Representation on Growth Rate in KVS Scheme.

In the bar graph as shown below in Fig. (**29**), increasing result from the year 2009 to 2013 can be observed.

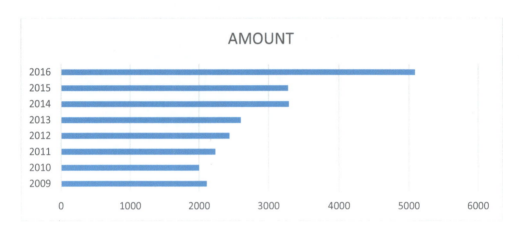

Fig. (29). Tentative Amount Allocation in KVS.

It was observed that, during the year 2009-2015, a consistent growth and increasing return have been observed. Our prediction during the year 2016 has a bit higher amount which we found favourable and align with the results.

Applying soft computing based OCBA technique, the result for Kendriya Vidyalaya Sangathan (KVS) is shown in the Fig. (**30**). The x-axis represents the several generations and y-axis represents the Probability of Correct Selection. Simulation results show the highest peak with Rs. 5177 Crores at the 1700 Generations. After this point, the probability reaches to 1, and so it will not be considered for our allocation.

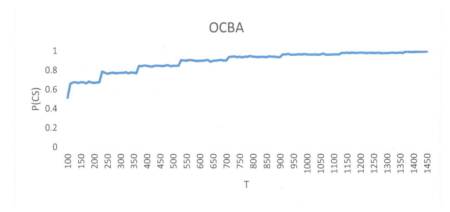

Fig. (30). Amount allocated in KVS scheme using OCBA Technique.

Fig. (**31**), shows an expression of EA technique for computing the growth rate. It is observed that the graph reaches at the level of 3800 generations after which it becomes constant.

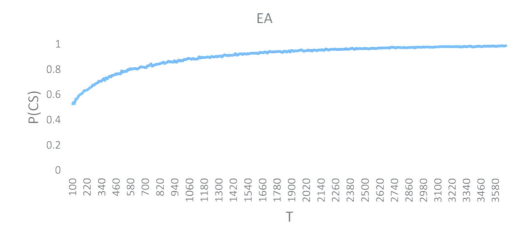

Fig. (31). Amount allocated in KVS scheme using EA Technique.

Table **14** represents the computation of growth rate using soft computing technique. Finally, the average of the three techniques OCBA, EA, and GA is considered and the final average amount is allocated to be Rs. 5149.33 Crores which is near about the predicted growth rate amount Rs. 5087.26. After averaging what we get is the predicted number which we proceed for the allocation of the fund in that scheme.

Table 14. Average Predicted Amount Allocation in KVS Scheme.

Technique	Predicted Amount	Final Average Amount Allocation
Growth Rate	5087.26 Crores	Rs. 5149.33 Crores
OCBA	5177 Crores	
EA	5149 Crores	
GA	5122 Crores	

4.7.3. Scheme 3: Central Tibetan School Society Administration

Scheme 3 represents Central Tibetan School Society Administration where Rs.38 Crores amount was allocated for development purposes during the year 2009. Taking this as a base, we find a growth rate percentage of 4.78% with an allocation of Rs. 39.82 Crores in 2010. During the year 2011, the amount allocated was increased up to Rs. 45 Crores with a growth rate of 13%. In the year 2012, the amount allocated reached the level of Rs. 49 Crores which generated 8.88% growth rate. During the year 2013, the amount allocated was Rs. 52.14 Crores with an increase of 6.408%. During the year 2014, the fund allocation has been increased to Rs. 55.85 Crores which gave the growth rate (%) 7.11. But during the year 2015, due to some reasons, the Growth Rate (%) denominated and it reached the level of -9.99% against the amount allocation Rs. 50 Crores. According to the prediction during the year 2016, the growth rate (%) was found to be 3.99 which shows the positive sign of allocation procedure as shown in Table **15**.

Table 15. Predicted and Year wise price allocation in Central Tibetan School Society Administration Scheme.

YEAR	AMOUNT	Growth Rate (%)
2009	38	
2010	39.82	4.78
2011	45	13
2012	49	8.88
2013	52.14	6.408
2014	55.85	7.11
2015	50	-9.99
2016	51.992	3.99

The graphical representation of Table **15** is shown in Fig. (**32**), where we find that after a denominated start a sudden growth was experienced during the year 2011 up to the year 2013. During the year 2013-2014, minimum growth rate was observed and a sudden downfall was experienced during the year 2015. In 2016, the prediction of budget allocation reached Rs. 51.992 Crores.

The expenditure of budget of Central Tibetan School Society Administration is shown as a bar graph in Fig. (**33**) which represents a reasonable increase in folding in the base year 2009. The fund allocation decreases in the year 2010. After that, more fund was spent during the year 2011 which gradually decreased, and during the year 2015, it reached at the level of Rs. 50 Crores. So, to achieve a reasonable increase in growth rate (%), the predicted amount can be spent during the year 2016 is Rs. 51.992 Crores which result positive.

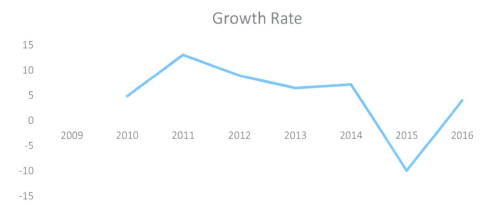

Fig. (32). Graphical Representation of Growth Rate.

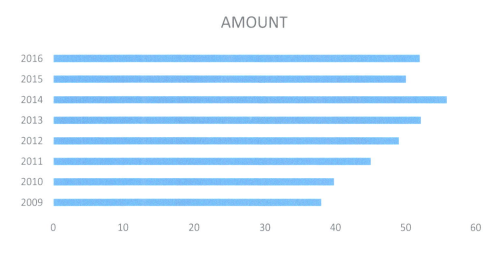

Fig. (33). Tentative Amount Allocation for Central Tibetan School Society Administration (CTSSA).

Fig. (**34**) represents that the growth rate has some increments relative to the previous year. The amount allocated here is efficiency based. The price was set up for the next year budget allocation using the previous year's budget efficiency. Using OCBA technique, we found a very considerable hike in the beginning, and after reaching the level of 740 generations the highest peak was achieved. After some generations, the increase got a negligible change and settled to a constant value.

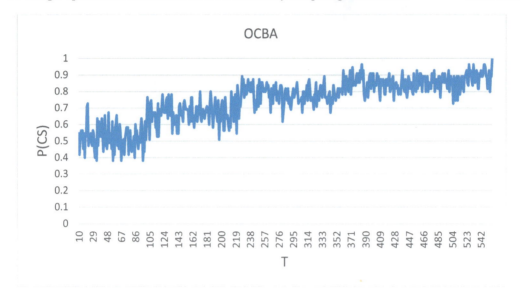

Fig. (34). Amount Allocation under OCBA Technique.

Then, we used another technique to compute the budget allocation which ended with the same results as we found in OCBA technique. Fig. (**35**) represents the results of EA method in which peak was reached at 1155 generations. Then the peak diminishes, and after some period, it reached to a constant level and so it was exempted.

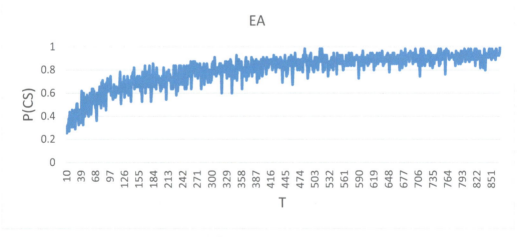

Fig. (35). Amount Allocation under EA Technique.

Table **16** represents the comparison between the OCBA, EA, and the GA method.

We concluded that the final average amount allocated is Rs. 53.17 Crores which is near about the predicted growth rate amount of Rs. 51.992 Crores. So, it is taken for the amount allocated to that scheme.

Table 16. Predicted Amount Allocation in CTSSA.

Technique	Predicted Amount	Final Average Amount Allocation
Growth Rate	51.992 Crores	Rs. 53.17 Crores
OCBA	53 Crores	
EA	56 Crores	
GA	52.14 Crores	

4.7.4. Scheme 4: Scheme for Setting Up 6000 Model Schools

The Government has a plan for setting up 6000 Model Schools. Table **17** shows that government spent Rs. 350 Crores during the year 2009. Assuming it as the base value, we found 21.42% of growth rate during the year 2010 with allocated amount of Rs. 425 Crores. During the year 2011, it was increased to amount of Rs. 1200 Crores. The funds assigned to model schools were decreased to the amount of Rs. 1 Crore and so there was a deficit of -99.41%. The allocation of the amount for model schools got more diminished and reached the level of Rs. 1 Crore in 2015 and so probably the growth rate is predicted at -56.69% during the year 2016.

Table 17. Year Wise Amount Allocation.

YEAR	AMOUNT	Growth Rate (%)
2009	350	
2010	425	21.42
2011	1200	182.35
2012	1080	-10
2013	1000	-7
2014	1200	20
2015	1	-99.41
2016	0.433	-56.69

Fig. (**36**) represents the growth rate (%) where we found that during the year 2011 it reached the apex. Comparatively, from 2010 to the year 2015, the performance of the scheme Growth Rate (%) even reached to -99.41%. So, the allocation of the fund during the year 2016 which is predicted to be Rs. 0.433 Crores is quite low.

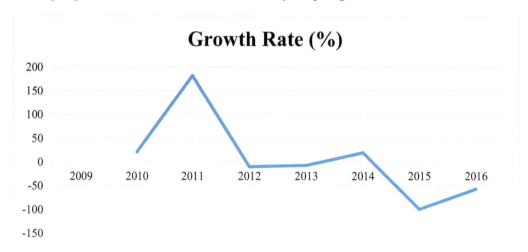

Fig. (36). Graphical Representation for Setting up 6000 Model School.

Fig. (**37**) shows the bar graph where we find the budget amount for 6000 model schools which was minimum during the year 2009 and got a hike during the year 2011 and year 2014. During the year 2015, the allocated amount reached to the least level, which was Rs. 1 Crore. The primary cause was to assign the least amount for the completion of many school buildings and the least number of schools is needed to be made. Therefore, the predicted amount for 2016 has been taken the least.

Fig. (37). Tentative amounts in 6000 model school.

Fig. (**38**) shown below is for the OCBA Technique. At the beginning, the generation started at near about probability 0.5 and gradually increased up to '1'. At 1125 iterations we get the highest peak, and the generated amount was allocated to be Rs. 0.443 crores.

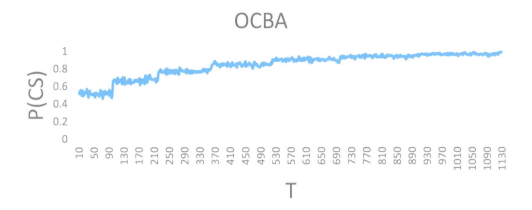

Fig. (38). Amount Allocation using OCBA Technique.

By using the EA method, the result produced was near about the same as we found in OCBA technique. In EA, the probability reached at the level of 1 with very few peaks and after 1535 generations, peaks decreases are shown in Fig. (**39**). So, after this the calculation is forgone.

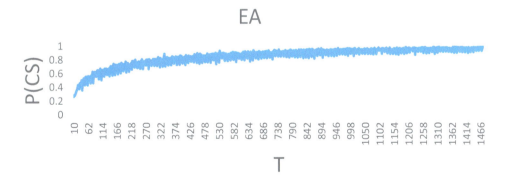

Fig. (39). Amount Allocation using EA Technique.

After a comparative study in Table **18**, we found that the predicted value through OCBA technique was Rs. 0.443 Crores, through the EA method the amount was Rs. 0.441 Crores and through the GA process the amount was Rs. 0.439 Crores.

As a conclusion, we found a final average fund allocation which is of Rs. 0.441 Crores.

Table 18. Predicted Amount Allocation for setting up 6000 model school.

Technique	Predicted Amount	Final Average Amount Allocation
Growth Rate	0.433 Crores	Rs. 0.441 Crores
OCBA	0.443 Crores	
EA	0.441 Crores	
GA	0.439 Crores	

4.7.5. Scheme 5: Rashtriya Madhyamik Shiksha Abhiyan (RMSA)

Table **19** represents the year wise allocation of RSMA scheme. During the year 2009, the allocated amount was Rs. 1700 Crores which was increased during the year 2010 and it resulted in the growth rate (%) of 42.58. During the year 2011, the allocated amount was Rs. 3124 Crores which achieved the growth rate of 28.88%, consequently. During the year 2012, the fund assigned for the development of RMSA was Rs.3983 Crores which achieved the growth rate 27.49%. After this downfall in growth rate started and growth rate was 25.53% against allocated amount of Rs. 5000 Crores during the year 2013. In continuation, year 2014 to the year 2015, the downfall was observed more. So the predicted value for the year 2016 is Rs. 1310 Crores and having a diminished growth rate of -3.19%.

Table 19. Year Wise Amount Allocation for RMSA.

YEAR	AMOUNT	Growth Rate (%)
2009	1700	
2010	2423.9	42.58
2011	3124	28.88
2012	3983	27.49
2013	5000	25.53
2014	3565	-28.7
2015	1353.98	-62.02
2016	1310	-3.19

The growth rate (%) is shown in Fig. (**40**), where we find that Rashtriya Madhyamik Shiksha Abhiyan (RMSA) has a continuous down fall in the growth rate (%). But the predicted allocation of the fund during the year 2016 had a good effect on the growth rate but the deficit was not entirely set out.

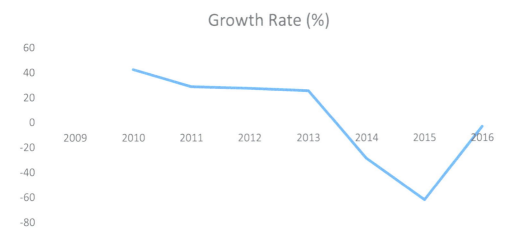

Fig. (40). Graphical Representation of growth rate for RMSA Scheme.

In Fig. (**41**), the allocated amount during the year 2009 increases up to the year 2013 but gradually we find a decrease till the year 2015. The predicted amount during the year 2016 has also been kept low as Rs. 1310 Crores but it is anticipated that the growth rate (%) must increase.

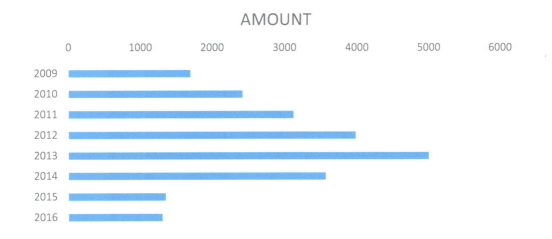

Fig. (41). Tentative Amount Allocation for RMSA.

In Fig. (**42**), the interim fund in RMSA scheme is given where a sudden increase is observed in the beginning using OCBA technique. Then it gets stagnant, but the problem of allocation effects of the year 2015 and 2016 is sorted out. At 1280 generation, we get the highest probability, and after that, the less satisfactory result is perceived so after this the calculation is thought to be negligible.

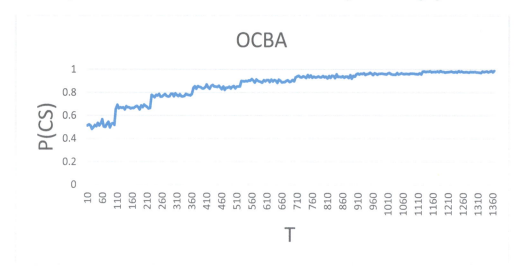

Fig. (42). Amount Allocation using OCBA Technique.

Fig. (**43**) represents the EA technique. In EA, the probability output gradually increases, and it takes 3470 Generations for the probability to reach its maximum. After that the iterations are stopped.

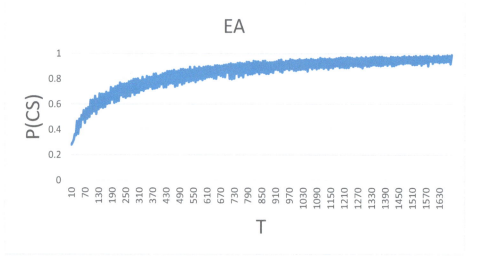

Fig. (43). Amount Allocation using EA Technique.

Table **20** represents the comparison between techniques like OCBA, EA, and GA from where we get predicted values such as Rs. 1257 Crores, Rs. 1339 Crores and Rs. 1320 Crores. The final fund allocation is calculated as average of these values comes out to be Rs. 1305 Crores, which reaches up to the growth rate amount predicted to be Rs. 1310 Crores.

Table 20. Predicted amount Allocation in RMSA.

Technique	Predicted Amount	Final Average Amount Allocation
Growth Rate	1310 Crores	Rs. 1305 Crores
OCBA	1257 Crores	
EA	1339 Crores	
GA	1320 Crores	

The result shows that there is very less increment for the years of 2015-2016 and as a result less priority is given to this scheme for the allocation of amount.

4.7.6. Scheme 6: Navodaya Vidyalaya Samiti (NVS)

Scheme 6 is for the Navodaya Vidyalaya Samiti (NVS). Table **21** represents the year wise allocation from 2009 to 2015. In 2009, the allocated fund was Rs. 1641.29 Crores which was increased during the year 2010 and reached at the level of Rs. 1755 Crores with a growth rate of (%) 6.95. In the year 2011, the amount was allocated Rs. 1608.8 Crores but the Growth Rate (%) was diminished and it reached at the level of -8.35%. In the year 2012, the amount spent was Rs. 1701.05 Crores and it produced 5.93% of growth rate. In the year 2013, the amount paid was Rs. 1748.29 Crores and growth rate was 2.77%. During the year 2014, the amount paid was Rs. 2038.4 Crores with a growth rate of 16.59%. We observe a downfall during the year 2015 when more amount was allocated, but the resultant growth rate was 1.108%. So, to compensate with the situation, the predicted fund is certainly significant and came out to be Rs. 2129.14 Crores and thus the growth rate was increased at the level of 3.3%.

Table 21. Year wise Amount allocated in NVS Scheme.

YEAR	AMOUNT	Growth Rate (%)
2009	1641.29	
2010	1755.4	6.95
2011	1608.8	-8.35
2012	1701.05	5.93
2013	1748.29	2.77

(Table 21) contd.....

YEAR	AMOUNT	Growth Rate (%)
2014	2038.4	16.59
2015	2061	1.108
2016	2129.14	3.3

In Fig. (**44**), the growth rate (%) is taken on the graph for year-wise budget allocation for NVS scheme. It was observed that the figure was getting a nadir point in the year 2011 and its zenith in the year 2014. During the year 2015, it again begins to diminish. But the predicted amount for 2016 made a significant growth rate (%) and increased during the year 2016.

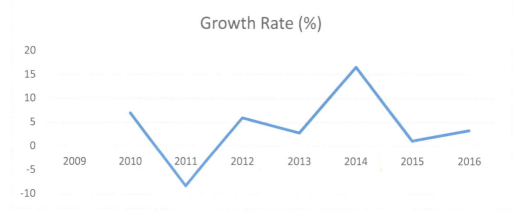

Fig. (44). Graphical Representation of Growth Rate for NVS Schema.

In Fig. (**45**), bar graph represents the minimum allocated amount during the year 2011 and maximum amount in the year 2016 which resulted in the final upgrading of growth rate (%). We found that, in the year 2010, the amount allocated to spend on the welfare of NVS was Rs. 1755.4 Crores and then the price decreased during the year 2011, and again during the year 2012, the allocated amount was increased which gave a positive result. During the year 2013, the amount spent was Rs. 1748.29 Crores which created a sudden growth during the year 2014. In 2015, the growth rate decreases suddenly even after allocating a good amount. In 2016, the predicted amount was sufficiently accurate and the growth rate made a positive turn due to this.

In Fig. (**46**), the graph represents the simulation of OCBA technique where we have tried to find out the probability of correct selection. In the beginning, we found sudden jerks in the probability, but after 1340 generations, it became equal to probability 1. This result is obtained through OCBA technique.

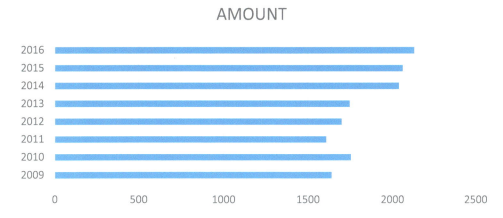

Fig. (45). Tentative Amount Allocation in NVS.

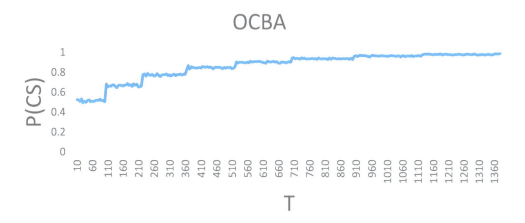

Fig. (46). Amount Allocation using OCBA Technique.

Fig. (**47**) represents the EA method where we have tried to find out the probability of correct selection for the simulation. We observed the highest peak at the point of 3723 generations. After that, the Generation results are close to 1. So it is not considered for further processing.

Table **22**, represents the predicted amount using all three techniques OCBA, EA, and GA. The predicted amount through OCBA technique is of Rs. 2013 Crores, through EA method the predicted amount is of Rs. 2179 Crores and through the GA process the predicted amount is of Rs. 2120 Crores. The average value is considered for final allocation comes out to be Rs. 2104 Crores which is comparatively closer to the growth rate Rs. 2129.14 Crores.

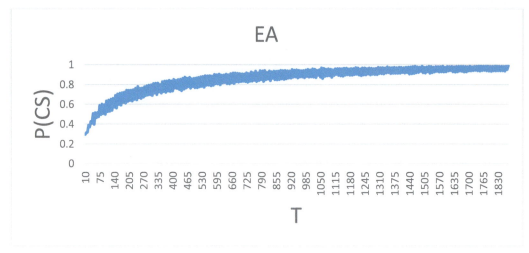

Fig. (47). Amount Allocation using EA Technique.

Table 22. Predicted Amount Allocation for NVS Scheme.

Technique	Predicted Amount	Final Average Amount Allocation
Growth Rate	2129.14 Crores	Rs. 2104 Crores
OCBA	2013 Crores	
EA	2179 Crores	
GA	2120 Crores	

The result shows that there are very less increments for the year of 2015-16 so that less priority is given to this scheme for the allocation of amount.

4.8. OUTPUT OF BUDGET ALLOCATION

The result is prepared according to the graphical representation of growth rate. The high growth rate shows more top priority for budget allocation. According to the survey, the ranking is performed on the different schemes. The Growth Rate is assumed as a parameter for the assignment dominantly. There are 21 projects and ranking is given to the major schemes in the secondary education as shown in Table **23**.

Table 23. Ranking and Selection Process for different scheme.

Project Optimization Using Ranking and Selection	
SCHEME	**Ranking and Selection Priority**
National Council Of Educational Research And Training (NCERT)	7

(Table 23) contd.....

Project Optimization Using Ranking and Selection	
SCHEME	Ranking and Selection Priority
Kendriya Vidyalaya Sangathan (KVS)	9
Navodaya Vidyalaya Samiti (NVS)	8
Rashtriya Madhyamik Shiksha Abhiyan (RMSA)	8
Scheme for setting up of 6000 model school at block level	7
Information and Communication Technology in schools	4
Integrated Education for disabled children	4
Inclusive education for the disabled at secondary school (IEDSS)	4
National Institute of open schooling	4
Access and Equity	7
Central Tibetan Schools Society Administration	7
Vocationalisation of Education	4
Scheme for universal access and quality at the secondary stage SUCCESS	4
National scheme for incentive to girls for secondary education SUCCESS	4
National Merit Scholarship Scheme	4
New Model School	4
Upgrading 2000 KGBVs residential schools, hostel/girls hostel	4
Scheme for construction and running of girls hostels	4
Appointment of language teacher	4
National means-cum merit scholarship for class 9 to 12	4
Other programs	7

Table **23** shows the allocation of the amount in the different schemes by equations 47, 48, 49, 50, and 51 according to the various projects. The output presented in Table **24** is for the overall budget. Fig. (**48**) represents the ranking of the schemes according to the prioritization.

Table **24** shows the allocated amount for different schemes in the secondary education system. The fund allocation was made on priority basis where the higher priority schemes get allocated first. Here, the ranking is done in-between (1 to 9), in our convention 9 is the topmost priority. We first allocate the amount in highest priority schemes. After that, taking base as a 30% of the total fund, we allocate the amount in the priority 8. For priority '7' allocation is done according to 20% base. The rest amount is allocated using EA technique according to the requirement in that scheme. The system where no money is allocated, is considered as a close scheme. The allocation is prepared according to the obligation, and it is observed that the calculated predicted amount seems to be close to the current government budget allocation.

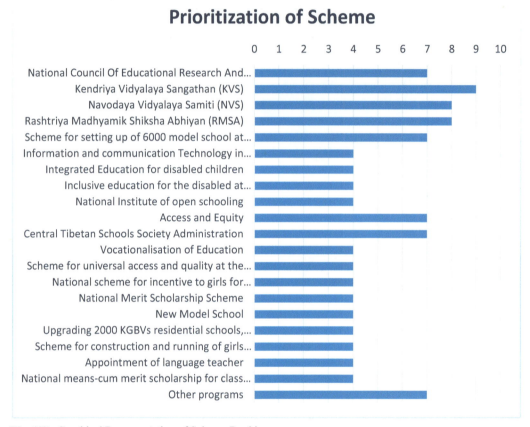

Fig. (48). Graphical Representation of Scheme Ranking.

Table 24. Amount Allocation in the Different Schemes.

	Budget allocation in different Schemes					
SCHEME	Ranking and Selection Priority	The amount allocated using the Equal Allocation Technique	30% of Amount Allocation	20% of Amount Allocation	Rest of Amount Allocation using Equal Allocation	Overall Budget Allocation in Secondary Education
National Council Of Educational Research And Training (NCERT)	7			247		247

(Table 24) contd.....

Budget allocation in different Schemes						
SCHEME	Ranking and Selection Priority	The amount allocated using the Equal Allocation Technique	30% of Amount Allocation	20% of Amount Allocation	Rest of Amount Allocation using Equal Allocation	Overall Budget Allocation in Secondary Education
Kendriya Vidyalaya Sangathan (KVS)	9	4431.0062			718.32	5149.32
Navodaya Vidyalaya Samiti (NVS)	8		1329.30		774.7247	2104.025
Rashtriya Madhyamik Shiksha Abhiyan (RMSA)	8		1304.33			1304.33
Scheme for setting up of 6000 model school at block level	7			0.441		0.441
Information and Communication Technology in schools	4					Closed
Integrated Education for disabled children	4					Closed
Inclusive education for the disabled at secondary school (IEDSS)	4					Closed
National Institute of open schooling	4					Closed
Access and Equity	7			1		1
Central Tibetan Schools Society Administration	7			53.17		53.17
Vocationalisation of Education	4					Closed
Scheme for universal access and quality at the secondary stage SUCCESS	4					Closed
National scheme for incentive to girls for secondary education SUCCESS	4					Closed
National Merit Scholarship Scheme	4					Closed
New Model School	4					Closed

(Table 24) contd.....

Budget allocation in different Schemes						
SCHEME	Ranking and Selection Priority	The amount allocated using the Equal Allocation Technique	30% of Amount Allocation	20% of Amount Allocation	Rest of Amount Allocation using Equal Allocation	Overall Budget Allocation in Secondary Education
Upgrading 2000 KGBVs residential schools, hostel/girls hostel	4					Closed
Scheme for construction and running of girls hostels	4					Closed
Appointment of language teacher	4					Closed
National means-cum merit scholarship for class 9 to 12	4					Closed
Other programs	7			2.74		2.74
TOTAL						Rs.8862.026

CONCLUDING REMARKS

There are various methods available for budget allocation and optimization, but among those techniques, the soft computing based budget allocation and optimization has its importance and effectiveness. In the optimization phase, the budget is allocated regarding ranking and the selection is based on prioritization where the schemes which need more fund (according to the previous survey report) are given the priority for the allocation of money. The projects where funds are underutilized or completely initialized have been observed, and the distribution has been performed with precaution or shut down according to its importance. In the distribution phase, the mathematically based fund allocation is compared with the soft computing based distribution, and the result is concluded by averaging the product of both technologies.

CONSENT FOR PUBLICATION

Not applicable.

CONFLICT OF INTEREST

This presentation certifies that authors have no affiliations with or involvement in any organization or entity with any financial interest (such as honoraria, educational grants, participation in speakers' bureaus, membership, employment, consultancies, stock ownership, or other equity interest; and expert testimony or patent-licensing arrangements), or Non-financial interest (such as personal or professional relationships, affiliations, knowledge or beliefs) in the subject matter or materials discussed in this manuscript.

ACKNOWLEDGEMENTS

We would like to thank Dr. M. K. Mishra, Vice-Chancellor, B.I.T. Mesra, Ranchi, for encouraging and providing us with resources and study materials. We also thank our family members for their patience, inspiration and allowing us to devote time to this work without which this work wouldn't have been possible.

Finally, we would like to acknowledge the publisher of this book "Bentham Science Publishers" for its wide circulation and making a provision for this article to reach every corner of the world.

REFERENCES

[1]   N.A. Pujowidianto, L.H. Lee, C.H. Chen, and C.M. Yap, "Optimal computing budget allocation for constrained optimization", *Winter Simulation Conference,* 2009
        [http://dx.doi.org/10.1109/WSC.2009.5429660]

[2]   H. Al-Battaineh, and S. AbouRizk, "Optimization of intermediate-level budget allocation using a genetic algorithm", *Int. J. Arch. Eng. Constr.,* vol. 2, no. 3, 2013.
        [http://dx.doi.org/10.7492/IJAEC.2013.014]

[3]   J.D. Gibbons, I. Olkin, and M. Sobel, "An introduction to ranking and selection", *Am. Stat.,* vol. 33, no. 4, 1979.

APPENDIX A

ALLOCATION OCBA

Public Class Allocation_OCBA

```
{

public Allocation_OCBA()

{}

public void run()

{

int i; int ADD_BUDGET=10;

double s_mean[]={100f, 200f, 300f, 400f, 500f};

double s_var[]= {10f, 20f, 40f, 50f, 60f};

int n[]={10}; int an[]={20};

optimal_cba(SA_mean, SA_var, 5, n, ADD_BUDGET, an, 1);

for(i=0;i<5;i++)

{

System.out.println("The budget allocation " + i +" is " + an[i]);

n[i] += an[i];

}

System.out.println("\n");

}


public int optimal_cba(double SA_mean[], double SA_var[], int nd, int n[], int add_budget,int an[], int type)

{
```

```
int i;

int b, s;

int t_budget,t1_budget;

int morerun[]= new int[nd];

int more_alloc = 0; /* 1:Yes; 0:No */

double t_s_mean[] = new double[nd];

double ratio[] = new double[nd];

double ratio_s,temp;

if (type == 1) /*MIN problem*/

{

for(i=0; i<nd; i++) t_s_mean[i] = s_mean[i];

}

else

{

for(i=0; i<nd; i++) t_s_mean[i] = (-1)*s_mean[i]; }

t_budget = add_budget;

for(i=0; i<nd; i++)

t_budget+=n[i];

b=best(t_s_mean, nd);

s=second_best(t_s_mean, nd, b);

ratio[s]=1.0f;

for(i=0;i<nd;i++)

if(i!=s && i!=b)

{

temp=(t_s_mean[b]-t_s_mean[s])/(t_s_mean[b]-t_s_mean[i]);

ratio[i]=temp*temp*s_var[i]/s_var[s];
```

```
}
temp=0;
for(i=0;i<nd;i++) if(i!=b) temp+=(ratio[i]*ratio[i]/s_var[i]);
ratio[b]=(float) Math.sqrt(s_var[b]*temp); /* calculate Nb */
for(i=0;i<nd;i++) morerun[i]=1;
t1_budget=t_budget;
do
{
more_alloc=0;
ratio_s=0.0f;
for(i=0;i<nd;i++)
if(morerun[i] == 1) ratio_s+=ratio[i];
for(i=0;i<nd;i++)
if(morerun[i] == 1)
{
an[i]=(int)(t1_budget/ratio_s*ratio[i]);
if(an[i]<n[i]) {
an[i]=n[i];
morerun[i]=0;
more_alloc=1;
}}
if(more_alloc == 1)
{
t1_budget=t_budget;
for(i=0;i<nd;i++) if(morerun[i]!= 1) t1_budget-=an[i];
}}
```

```
while(more_alloc== 1);

t1_budget=an[0];

for(i=1;i<nd;i++) t1_budget+=an[i];

an[b]+=(t_budget-t1_budget);

for(i=0;i<nd;i++) an[i]-=n[i];

return b;

}

public int best(double t_s_mean[], int nd)

{

int i, min_index;

min_index=0;

for(i=0;i<nd;i++)

{

if(t_s_mean[i]<t_s_mean[min_index])

{ min_index=i;

}}

return min_index;

}

public int second_best(double t_s_mean[], int nd, int b)

{ int i, second_index;

if(b==0) second_index=1;

else second_index=0;

for(i=0;i<nd;i++) {

if(t_s_mean[i]<t_s_mean[second_index] && i!=b)

{ second_index=i;

}}
```

```
return second_index;

} public static void main(String argv[]) {

AOCBA a = new AOCBA();

a.run();

}

}
```

Applet Window Code for Simulation

```
public class AppletFrame extends JApplet {

private int PREFERRED_WIDTH = 800;

private int PREFERRED_HEIGHT = 800;

Border          loweredBorder          =          new          CompoundBorder(new
SoftBevelBorder(SoftBevelBorder.LOWERED),  new  EmptyBorder(5,5,5,5));

private JPanel panel = null;

private String resourceName = null;

public AppletFrame(String resourceName) {

panel = new JPanel();

panel.setLayout(new BorderLayout());

this.resourceName = resourceName;

}

public String getResourceName()

{ return resourceName;

}

public JPanel getAppletFrame()

{ return panel;}

public void mainImpl()

{ JFrame frame = new JFrame(getName());
```

```java
frame.getContentPane().setLayout(new BorderLayout());

frame.getContentPane().add(getAppletFrame(), BorderLayout.CENTER);

getAppletFrame().setPreferredSize(new                Dimension(PREFERRED_WIDTH,
PREFERRED_HEIGHT));

frame.pack();

frame.show();

}

public JPanel createHorizontalPanel(boolean threeD)

{

JPanel p = new JPanel();

p.setLayout(new BoxLayout(p, BoxLayout.X_AXIS));

p.setAlignmentY(TOP_ALIGNMENT);

p.setAlignmentX(LEFT_ALIGNMENT);

if(threeD)

{ p.setBorder(loweredBorder);

} return p;

}

public JPanel createVerticalPanel(boolean threeD)

{

JPanel p = new JPanel();

p.setLayout(new BoxLayout(p, BoxLayout.Y_AXIS));

p.setAlignmentY(TOP_ALIGNMENT);

p.setAlignmentX(LEFT_ALIGNMENT);

if(threeD) {

p.setBorder(loweredBorder); }

return p;
```

```
}
public static JPanel createPaneV(JComponent pane1, JComponent pane2)

{

JPanel pane = new JPanel();

pane.setLayout(new BoxLayout(pane, BoxLayout.Y_AXIS));

pane1.setAlignmentX(Component.LEFT_ALIGNMENT);

pane2.setAlignmentX(Component.LEFT_ALIGNMENT);

pane.add(pane1);

pane.add(pane2);

return pane;

}

public static JPanel createPaneH(JComponent pane1, JComponent pane2)

{

JPanel pane = new JPanel();

pane.setLayout(new BoxLayout(pane, BoxLayout.X_AXIS));

pane1.setAlignmentY(Component.LEFT_ALIGNMENT);

pane2.setAlignmentY(Component.LEFT_ALIGNMENT);

pane.add(pane1);

pane.add(pane2);

return pane;

}

public void init()

{ getContentPane().setLayout(new BorderLayout());

getContentPane().add(getAppletFrame(), BorderLayout.CENTER);

}

public void onRun(SimulationPane sP)
```

```
{}
public int onTic(SimulationPane sP)
{ return 0; }
public static void main(String[] args)
{ AppletFrame sim = new AppletFrame("asad");
sim.mainImpl();
}
}
```

Simulation Pane Code for simulation

```
public class SimulationPane
{
public JProgressBar progressBar1;
public JProgressBar progressBar2;
public JTextArea resultTextArea;
public UGraph graph;
javax.swing.Timer timer;
int maxSimulation = 10000;
public AppletFrame simulationWindow;
public SimulationPane(AppletFrame sW)
{
simulationWindow = sW; }
void updateDragEnabled(boolean dragEnabled)
{
resultTextArea.setDragEnabled(dragEnabled);
}
public void setMaxSimulation(int nSize)
```

```
{

maxSimulation = nSize;

}

public JPanel createTextOut()

{

JPanel textWrapper = new JPanel();

textWrapper.setLayout(new BoxLayout(textWrapper, BoxLayout.X_AXIS));

resultTextArea = new TextOutArea();

textWrapper.add(new JScrollPane(resultTextArea));

return textWrapper;

}

public JPanel createProgress1(String str)

{

JLabel description = new JLabel(str);

progressBar1 = new JProgressBar(JProgressBar.HORIZONTAL, 0, maxSimulation)

{

public Dimension getPreferredSize()

{

return new Dimension(50, 10);

Dimension(super.getPreferredSize().width, super.getPreferredSize().height);

} };

return AppletFrame.createPaneH(description, progressBar1);

}

public JPanel createProgress2(String str1, String str2)

{

JLabel description1 = new JLabel(str1);
```

```java
JLabel description2 = new JLabel(str2);

return AppletFrame.createPaneH(description1, description2);

}

public JPanel createPanel(String strDesc1, String strDesc2, String strDesc3, String strDesc4,
int maxSim)

{

setMaxSimulation(maxSim);

JPanel textWrapper = createTextOut();

JPanel progress1 = createProgress1(" Total Replication Increment ");

JPanel progress2 = createProgress2(" ", " ");

JPanel leftBottom = AppletFrame.createPaneV(progress1, progress2);

JPanel left = AppletFrame.createPaneV(textWrapper, leftBottom);

graph = new UGraph();

graph.setMaxValues(maxSim, 1);

JLabel description1 = new JLabel(strDesc3);

JLabel description2 = new JLabel(strDesc4);

JPanel rightBottom = AppletFrame.createPaneV(description1, description2);

JPanel right = AppletFrame.createPaneV(graph, rightBottom);

JPanel center = AppletFrame.createPaneH(left, right);

JLabel title1 = new JLabel(strDesc1);

JLabel title2 = new JLabel(strDesc2);

JPanel top = AppletFrame.createPaneV(title1, title2);

return AppletFrame.createPaneV(top, center);

}

public void run()

{
```

```
if(timer == null)

{

if(progressBar1.getValue() == progressBar1.getMaximum())

{

progressBar1.setValue(0);

resultTextArea.setText("");

}

timer = new javax.swing.Timer(18, createTextLoadAction());

timer.start();

onRun();

}

}

public void stop()

{

if(timer != null)

{

timer.stop();

timer = null;

}}

public Action createTextLoadAction()

{

return new AbstractAction("text load action")

{ public void actionPerformed (ActionEvent e)

{

if(progressBar1.getValue() < progressBar1.getMaximum())

{
```

```
progressBar1.setValue(onTic());

graph.repaint();

}

else

{

if(timer != null)

{

110 Appendix A

timer.stop();

timer = null;

} } } };

}

private void onRun()

{

simulationWindow.onRun(this);

}

protected int onTic()

{

return simulationWindow.onTic(this);

}

class TextOutArea extends JTextArea

{

public TextOutArea()

{

super(null, 0, 0);

setEditable(false);
```

```
setText("");

}

public float getAlignmentX ()

{

return LEFT_ALIGNMENT;

}

public float getAlignmentY ()

{

return TOP_ALIGNMENT;

}

}

}
```

OCBA and EA Simulation Run

```
public class SimulationWindow_UniformTest extends AppletFrame

{

private static final long serialVersionUID = -1648721175751004369L;

Action loadAction;

Action stopAction;

SimulationPane Sim1;

SimulationPane Sim2;

public static void main(String[] args)

{

SimulationWindow_UniformTest    sim    =    new    SimulationWindow_UniformTest();
sim.mainImpl();

}

public SimulationWindow_UniformTest()
```

```
{

super("SimulationWindow");

Sim1 = new SimulationPane(this);

Sim2 = new SimulationPane(this);

JPanel paneSim1 = Sim1.createPanel(" Using OCBA", " Description1", " Description2", "
Description3", 9900);

JPanel paneSim2 = Sim2.createPanel(" Using Equal Allocation", " Description1", "
Description2", " Description3", 9900);

JPanel pane1 = createPaneV(paneSim1, paneSim2);

JPanel pane2 = createPaneH(createLoadButton(), createStopButton());

getAppletFrame().add(pane1, BorderLayout.CENTER);

getAppletFrame().add(pane2, BorderLayout.SOUTH);

}

public JButton createLoadButton()

{

loadAction = new AbstractAction("Simulation start")

{

public void actionPerformed(ActionEvent e)

{

Sim1.run();

Sim2.run();

loadAction.setEnabled(false);

stopAction.setEnabled(true);

} };

return createButton(loadAction);

}

public JButton createStopButton()
```

```
{
stopAction = new AbstractAction("Stop")
{
public void actionPerformed(ActionEvent e)
{
Sim1.stop();
Sim2.stop();
loadAction.setEnabled(true);
stopAction.setEnabled(false);
}};
return createButton(stopAction);
}
public JButton createButton(Action a)
{
JButton b = new JButton();
b.putClientProperty("displayActionText", Boolean.TRUE);
b.setAction(a);
return b;
}
Integer inT = 50;
Integer ocbaT = 50;
Integer equalT = 50;
Simulation_UniformOCBA ocba = null;
Simulation_UniformEqual equal = null;
public void onRun(SimulationPane sP)
{
```

```
if(Sim1 == sP)

{

ocba = new Simulation_UniformOCBA();

ocba.setExperimentMax(9900);

}

else

if(Sim2 == sP)

{

equal = new Simulation_UniformEqual();

equal.setExperimentMax(9900);

}}

public int onTic(SimulationPane sP)

{

if(Sim1 == sP)

{

ocbaT += inT;

if(ocba.run(ocbaT))

sP.graph.setCheckPoint(ocbaT-inT, ocba.probCorrectSelection, ocbaT.toString());

else

sP.graph.setPoint(ocbaT-inT, ocba.probCorrectSelection);

return ocbaT;

}

else

if(Sim2 == sP)

{

equalT += inT;
```

```
if(equal.run(equalT))

sP.graph.setCheckPoint(equalT-inT, equal.probCorrectSelection, equalT.toString());

else

sP.graph.setPoint(equalT-inT, equal.probCorrectSelection);

return equalT;

}

return 0;

}

}
```

Optimal Computing Budget Allocation Simulation

```
public class OCBA

{

public Integer Replication = 0;

public Integer SumReplication = 0;

public int index;

public Double sumLocal = 0.0;

public Double mean = 0.0;

public Double variance =0.0;

public Double best = 0.0;

public UniformOCBA(int i){

index = i;

}

public double run() {

return (Math.random() * (21) - 10.5 + index);

}

public void runSimulation()
```

```
{

Double u[] = new Double[replication];

//Find mean

for(int i = 0; i < replication; i++)

{

Double d = run();

u[i] = d;

sumLocal += u[i];

}

sumreplication += replication;

mean = sumLocal/sumreplication;

//Find variance

for(int i = 0; i < replication; i++)

{

variance += (u[i] - mean)*(u[i] - mean);

}

if(replication > 1)

variance = variance/(sumreplication - 1);

}}

//Simulation_UniformOCBA

UniformOCBA sim[] = new UniformOCBA[10];

AOCBA OCBAMain = new AOCBA();

int experimentMax = 50000;

boolean b99 = false;

public Double probCorrectSelection = 0.0;

public Simulation_UniformOCBA()
```

```
{
for(int i = 0; i < 10; i++)
sim[i] = new UniformOCBA(i);
}
public void setExperimentMax(int max)
{
experimentMax = max;
}
public boolean run(int T)
{
for (int i=0; i<10;i++){
sim[i].best = 0.0;
}
for(Integer experiments = 0; experiments < experimentMax; experiments++)
{
for (int i=0; i<10;i++){
sim[i].mean = 0.0;
sim[i].sumLocal= 0.0;
sim[i].sumreplication = 0;
sim[i].replication = 10;
}
//RUN OCBA
double s_mean[]= new double[10];
double s_var[] = new double[10];
int n[] = new int[10];
int an[]= new int[10];
```

```
int sumreplication = 0;

int ADD_BUDGET=20;

while(sumreplication < T){

for(int i = 0; i < 10; i++){

sim[i].runSimulation();

s_mean[i] = sim[i].mean;

s_var[i] = sim[i].variance;

n[i] = sim[i].replication;

sumreplication += sim[i].replication;

}

OCBAMain.ocba(s_mean, s_var, 10, n, ADD_BUDGET, an, 1);

for(int i = 0; i < 10; i++){

sim[i].replication += an[i];

}

}

//find min(best)

int i, min_index;

min_index=0;

for(i=0;i<10;i++)

if(sim[i].mean < sim[min_index].mean)

min_index=i;

//Set best

sim[min_index].best++;

}

//find p{cs}

Double sum = 0.0;
```

```
for(int i=0;i<10;i++)

{

sum += sim[i].best;

}

//Text out

probCorrectSelection = sim[0].best/sum;

System.out.println("T = " + T + " " + "Sum = " + sum + " best = " + sim[0].best +" P{CS} =
" +" " + probCorrectSelection);

if(probCorrectSelection > 0.99 && !b99){

b99 = true;

return true;

}return false;}

public static void main(String argv[])

{

Simulation_UniformOCBA su = new Simulation_UniformOCBA();

for(Integer T = 200; T < 5000; T+=100)

if(su.run(T)) break;

}

}
```

Equal Allocation (EA) Simulation

```
public class EqualAllocation

{

public Integer replication = 0;

public Integer sumreplication = 0;

public int index;

public Double sumLocal = 0.0;
```

```java
public Double mean = 0.0;

public Double variance =0.0;

public Double best = 0.0;

public UniformEqual(int i){

index = i;

}

public double run ()

{

return (Math.random() * (21) - 10.5 + index);

}

public void runSimulation(){

Double u[] = new Double[replication];

//Find mean

for(int i = 0; i < replication; i++)

{

Double d = run();

u[i] = d;

sumLocal += u[i];

}

sumreplication += replication;

mean = sumLocal/sumreplication;

//Find variance

for(int i = 0; i < replication; i++)

variance += (u[i] - mean)*(u[i] - mean);

if(replication > 1)

variance = variance/(sumreplication - 1);
```

```
}

}

//Simulation_EqualAllocation

UniformEqual sim[] = new UniformEqual[10];

int experimentMax = 50000;

boolean b99 = false;

public Double probCorrectSelection = 0.0;

public Simulation_UniformEqual()

{

for(int i = 0; i < 10; i++)

sim[i] = new UniformEqual(i);

}

public void setExperimentMax(int max)

{

experimentMax = max;

}

public boolean run(int T)

{

for (int i=0; i<10;i++){

sim[i].best = 0.0;

}

for(Integer experiments = 0; experiments < experimentMax; experiments++)

{

for (int i=0; i<10;i++)

{

sim[i].mean = 0.0;
```

```
sim[i].sumLocal= 0.0;

sim[i].sumreplication = 0;

}
/* Equal Test Run*/

int sumreplication = 0;

while(sumreplication < T)

{

for(int i = 0; i < 10; i++)

{

sim[i].replication = T/10;

sim[i].runSimulation();

sumreplication += sim[i].replication; }}

//find min(best)

int i, min_index;

min_index=0;

for(i=0;i<10;i++)

if(sim[i].mean < sim[min_index].mean)

min_index=i;

//Set best

sim[min_index].best++;

}
//find p{cs}

Double sum = 0.0;

for(int i=0;i<10;i++)

{

sum += sim[i].best;
```

```
}
//Text out
probCorrectSelection = sim[0].best/sum;

System.out.println("T = " + T + " " + "Sum = " + sum + " best = " + sim[0].best +" P{CS} =
" +" " +probCorrectSelection);

if(probCorrectSelection > 0.99 && !b99)
{
b99 = true;
return true;
}
return false;
}
public static void main(String argv[])
{
Simulation_UniformEqual su = new Simulation_UniformEqual();
for(Integer T = 42000; T < 45000; T+=10)
if(su.run(T)) break;
}}
```

Graph Generation

```
public class UGraph extends JPanel
{
int maxPoint = 10000;
int xPoints[] = new int[maxPoint];
int yPoints[] = new int[maxPoint];
int nPoints = 0;
int checkPoint = -1;
```

```java
String checkStr = "";

int xMax = 0;

int yMax = 0;

Color barColor = new Color(0,0,255);

Rectangle rcChart = null;

public UGraph()

{

super();

}

public void setMaxValues(int mx, int my)

{

xMax = mx;

yMax = my;

}

public void setCheckPoint(int x, double y, String str)

{

Integer xNew;

Integer yNew;

xNew = (int)(x*((double)rcChart.width/xMax));

yNew = (int)(y*((double)rcChart.height/yMax));

checkPoint = xNew + 30;

checkStr = str;

setPoint(xNew, yNew);

setPoint(xNew, 0);

setPoint(xNew, yNew);

}
```

```
public void setPoint(int x, double y)

{Integer xNew;

Integer yNew;

yNew = (int)(y*((double)rcChart.height/yMax));

xNew = (int)(x*((double)rcChart.width/xMax));

setPoint(xNew, yNew);

} public void setPoint(int x, int y)

{ if(nPoints < maxPoint)

{ xPoints[nPoints] = rcChart.x + x;

yPoints[nPoints] = rcChart.y + rcChart.height - y;

nPoints++;

}}

public void setBarColor(Color c)

{ barColor = c;

} public void paintComponent(Graphics g)

{

super.paintComponent(g);

Graphics2D g2 = (Graphics2D) g;

Rectangle rc = this.getBounds();

int newWidth = rc.width - 50;

newWidth /= 10;

newHeight /= 10;

rcChart = new Rectangle(25 + ((rc.width - 50) - newWidth*10)/2, 25 + ((rc.height - 50) - newHeight*10)/2,

newWidth*10, newHeight*10);

int newHeight = rc.height - 50;
```

```
g.setColor(new Color(255,255,255));

g.fillRect(rc.x, rc.y, rc.width, rc.height);

g.setColor(new Color(50,50,50));

g.draw3DRect(rc.x, rc.y, rc.width-2, rc.height-2, true);

g.drawString("p{cs}", 30, 20);

g.drawString("T", rc.width - 20, rc.height-30);

g.draw3DRect(rcChart.x, rcChart.y, rcChart.width, rcChart.height, true);

g.setColor(new Color(200,200,200));

Double pcs = 0.0;

Double pcsShow = 1.0;

Integer T = 0;

for(int x = 0; x < (rcChart.width); x+= (rcChart.width)/10)

{

.drawLine(rcChart.x+x, rcChart.y, rcChart.x+x, rcChart.y + rcChart.height);

g.drawString(T.toString(), rcChart.x+x, rcChart.height +rcChart.y+20);

T += xMax/10;

}

for(int y = 0; y < (rcChart.height); y+= (rcChart.height)/10)

{

String strP = String.format("%.1f", pcsShow);

g.drawLine(rcChart.x, rcChart.y+y, rcChart.x+rcChart.width, rcChart.y+y);

g.drawString(strP, rcChart.x-20, rcChart.y+y);

pcs += 0.1f;

pcsShow = (1.0 - pcs);

}

g.setColor(barColor);
```

```
g.drawPolyline(xPoints, yPoints, nPoints);

if(checkPoint > 0)

g.drawString(checkStr, checkPoint, rc.height-30);

}

}
```

APPENDIX B

SIMULATION OF MEAN AND STANDARD DEVIATION

```
public class mean extends HttpServlet

{

mean me=new mean();

me.setyear_2009(request.getParameter(com.budget.web.controller.frontcontroller.y_year_2009));

me.setyear_2010(request.getParameter(com.budget.web.controller.frontcontroller.y_year_2010));

me.setyear_2011(request.getParameter(com.budget.web.controller.frontcontroller.y_year_2011));

me.setyear_2012(request.getParameter(com.budget.web.controller.frontcontroller.y_year_2012));

me.setyear_2013(request.getParameter(com.budget.web.controller.frontcontroller.y_year_2013));
me.setyear_2014(request.getParameter(com.budget.web.controller.frontcontroller.y_year_2014));

me.setyear_2015(request.getParameter(com.budget.web.controller.frontcontroller.y_year_2015));

me.setnumber_of_year(request.getParameter(com.budget.web.controller.frontcontroller.n_number_of_year));

check(me,request,response);

}




public void check(mean me,HttpServletRequest request,HttpServletResponse response)
throws IOException, ServletException

{

String y_2009=null; String y_2010=null; String y_2011=null;

String y_2012=null; String y_2013=null; String y_2014=null;
```

```
String y_2015=null; String n_year=null;

Float mean, variance, sd, a, b, c, d, e, f, g, h, i;

Try

{

y_2009 = me.getyear_2009();

y_2010 = me.getyear_2010();

y_2011 = me.getyear_2011();

y_2012 = me.getyear_2012();

y_2013 = me.getyear_2013();

y_2014 = me.getyear_2014();

y_2015 = me.getyear_2015();

n_year = me.getnumber_of_year();

a                                                                    =
((Float.parseFloat(y_2009))+(Float.parseFloat(y_2010))+(Float.parseFloat(y_2011))+(Float.p
arseFloat(y_2012))+(Float.parseFloat(y_2013))+(Float.parseFloat(y_2014))+(Float.parseFloa
t(y_2015)));

mean= (a/(Float.parseFloat(n_year)));

// mean

System.out.println("mean =" +mean);

request.setAttribute("mean", mean);

// variance

b=mean-(Float.parseFloat(y_2009));

c=mean-(Float.parseFloat(y_2010));

d=mean-(Float.parseFloat(y_2011));

e=mean-(Float.parseFloat(y_2012));

f=mean-(Float.parseFloat(y_2013));

g=mean-(Float.parseFloat(y_2014));
```

```
h=mean-(Float.parseFloat(y_2015));

i=((float) Math.pow(b,2)+ (float) Math.pow(c,2)+(float) Math.pow(d,2)+

(float) Math.pow(e,2)+(float) Math.pow(f,2)+(float) Math.pow(g,2)+(float) Math.pow(h,2));

variance= (i/(Float.parseFloat(n_year)));

System.out.println("variance =" +variance);

request.setAttribute("variance",variance);

//Standard deviation

sd= (float) Math.sqrt(variance);

System.out.println("Standard deviation =" +sd);

request.setAttribute("sd",sd);

float Incremental_Budget= (((Float.parseFloat(y_2015))+sd));

System.out.println("Incremental_Budget =" +Incremental_Budget);

request.setAttribute("Incremental_Budget",Incremental_Budget);

RequestDispatcher
rd=request.getRequestDispatcher(com.budget.web.controller.frontcontroller.m_mean);

rd.forward(request,response);

} catch(Exception s)

{ System.out.println(s);

}}}
```

Calculation of Growth Rate

```
Public class fund extends HttpServlet

{

Private static final long serialVersionUID = 1L;

Protected void doPost (HttpServletRequest request, HttpServletResponse response) throws
ServletException, IOException {

Fundtable ti=new fundtable ();

ti.setpresent_year                                              (request.getParameter
```

(com.budget.web.controller.frontcontroller.P_present_year));

ti.setlast_year   (request.getParameter (com.budget.web.controller.frontcontroller.L_last_year));

ti.setnumber_of_year   (request.getParameter (com.budget.web.controller.frontcontroller.N_number_of_year));

Check (ti, request, response) ;}

Public void check (fundtable ti, HttpServletRequest request, HttpServletResponse response) throws IOException, ServletException {

String present=null; String last=null; String year=null;

Float growth_rate, a, b, d;

Try {present = ti.getpresent_year(); last= ti.getlast_year(); year= ti.getnumber_of_year();

a= ((Float.parseFloat(present))/(Float.parseFloat(last)));

b=1/(Float.parseFloat(year));

d=(float) Math.pow(a,b);

growth_rate=(d-1);

request.setAttribute("growth_rate", growth_rate);

float growth_rate_perct=growth_rate*100;

request.setAttribute("growth_rate_perct",growth_rate_perct);

float   Incremental_Budget=   (Float.parseFloat(present))*growth_rate; request.setAttribute("Incremental_Budget",Incremental_Budget);

float Budget_Allocation=Incremental_Budget+(Float.parseFloat(present));

request.setAttribute("Budget_Allocation",Budget_Allocation);

RequestDispatcher rd=request.getRequestDispatcher(com.budget.web.controller.frontcontroller.f_fund);

rd.forward(request,response); }

catch(Exception s) {}

}

}

Department Wise Budget Allocation

```
package com.budget.web.utility;

import java.io.IOException;

import java.io.PrintWriter;

import javax.servlet.RequestDispatcher;

import javax.servlet.ServletException;

import javax.servlet.annotation.WebServlet;

import javax.servlet.http.HttpServlet;

import javax.servlet.http.HttpServletRequest;

import javax.servlet.http.HttpServletResponse;

import com.budget.web.model.fundtable;

import com.budget.web.model.schemevalue;

public class optimization extends HttpServlet

{

private static final long serialVersionUID = 1L;

public optimization() {

super(); // TODO Auto-generated constructor stub

}

protected void doPost(HttpServletRequest request, HttpServletResponse response) throws
ServletException, IOException { // TODO Auto-generated method stub

schemevalue sv=new schemevalue();

sv.setpriority_value(request.getParameter(com.budget.web.controller.frontcontroller.p_value)
);

sv.setDepartment_value(request.getParameter(com.budget.web.controller.frontcontroller.D_v
alue));

sv.setAmount_value(request.getParameter(com.budget.web.controller.frontcontroller.A_value
));
```

```
sv.setpr_value1(request.getParameter(com.budget.web.controller.frontcontroller.p_value12));
sv.setp3(request.getParameter(com.budget.web.controller.frontcontroller.pro_value3));
sv.setp4(request.getParameter(com.budget.web.controller.frontcontroller.pro_value4));
sv.setp5(request.getParameter(com.budget.web.controller.frontcontroller.pro_value5));
sv.setp6(request.getParameter(com.budget.web.controller.frontcontroller.pro_value6));
sv.setp7(request.getParameter(com.budget.web.controller.frontcontroller.pro_value7));
sv.setp8(request.getParameter(com.budget.web.controller.frontcontroller.pro_value8));
sv.setp9(request.getParameter(com.budget.web.controller.frontcontroller.pro_value9));
sv.setp10(request.getParameter(com.budget.web.controller.frontcontroller.pro_value10));
sv.setp11(request.getParameter(com.budget.web.controller.frontcontroller.pro_value11));
sv.setp12(request.getParameter(com.budget.web.controller.frontcontroller.pro_value12));
sv.setp13(request.getParameter(com.budget.web.controller.frontcontroller.pro_value13));
sv.setp14(request.getParameter(com.budget.web.controller.frontcontroller.pro_value14));
sv.setp15(request.getParameter(com.budget.web.controller.frontcontroller.pro_value15));
sv.setp16(request.getParameter(com.budget.web.controller.frontcontroller.pro_value16));
sv.setp17(request.getParameter(com.budget.web.controller.frontcontroller.pro_value17));
sv.setp18(request.getParameter(com.budget.web.controller.frontcontroller.pro_value18));
sv.setp19(request.getParameter(com.budget.web.controller.frontcontroller.pro_value19));
sv.setp20(request.getParameter(com.budget.web.controller.frontcontroller.pro_value20));
sv.setp21(request.getParameter(com.budget.web.controller.frontcontroller.pro_value21));
response.setContentType("text/html");
PrintWriter out = response.getWriter();
out.print("<a href=\"home.jsp>");
System.out.println("YOUR APPLICATION HAS BEEN SAVED ");
check(sv,request,response);}
public void check(schemevalue sv,HttpServletRequest request,HttpServletResponse response)
```

```
throws IOException, ServletException

{

String M=null;

String dept_value=null;

String priority=null;

String pr1=null;

String pr3=null;

String pr4=null;

String pr5=null;

String pr6=null;

String pr7=null;

String pr8=null;

String pr9=null;

String pr10=null;

String pr11=null;

String pr12=null;

String pr13=null;

String pr14=null;

String pr15=null;

String pr16=null;

String pr17=null;

String pr18=null;

String pr19=null;

String pr20=null;

String pr21=null;

float a,M1,M2,b,c,d,e,f,g,h,i,j,k,l,m,n,o,p,q,r,s,t,u,v;
```

```
priority = sv.getpriority_value();
b=Float.parseFloat(priority);
pr1=sv.getpr_value1();
c=Float.parseFloat(pr1);
pr3=sv.getp3();
d=Float.parseFloat(pr3);
pr4=sv.getp4();
e=Float.parseFloat(pr4);
pr5=sv.getp5();
f=Float.parseFloat(pr5);
pr6=sv.getp6();
g=Float.parseFloat(pr6);
pr7=sv.getp7();
h=Float.parseFloat(pr7);
pr8=sv.getp8();
i=Float.parseFloat(pr8);
pr9=sv.getp9();
j=Float.parseFloat(pr9);
pr10=sv.getp10();
k=Float.parseFloat(pr10);
pr11=sv.getp11();
l=Float.parseFloat(pr11);
pr12=sv.getp12();
m=Float.parseFloat(pr12);
pr13=sv.getp13();
n=Float.parseFloat(pr13);
```

```
pr14=sv.getp14();

o=Float.parseFloat(pr14);

pr15=sv.getp15();

p=Float.parseFloat(pr15);

pr16=sv.getp16();

q=Float.parseFloat(pr16);

pr17=sv.getp17();

r=Float.parseFloat(pr17);

pr18=sv.getp18();

s=Float.parseFloat(pr18);

pr19=sv.getp19();

t=Float.parseFloat(pr19);

pr20=sv.getp20();

u=Float.parseFloat(pr20);

pr21=sv.getp21();

v=Float.parseFloat(pr21);

double[] num={b,c,d,e,f,g,h,i,j,k,l,m,n,o,p,q,r,s,t,u,v};

M = sv.getAmount_value();

System.out.println("Amount"+M);

M1=Float.parseFloat(M)/2;

System.out.println("Half Amount"+M1);

M2=(Float.parseFloat(M)-M1);

System.out.println("Another Amount"+M2);

dept_value = sv.getDepartment_value();

float a1= ((M2*20)/100);

System.out.println("20 percent amount" +a1);
```

```
float M3 = M2-a1;

float a4=((M3*30)/100);

System.out.println("30 percent amount" +a4);

float a5= M1+a1+M3;

System.out.println("total Amount" +a5);

float a6= M2-a1+a4;

System.out.println("Remaining Amount" +a6);

int count =0;

int count1=0;

int count2=0;

int count3=0;

for(int as=0;as<num.length;as++) {

if(num[as]<=10 && num[as]>=8){

count=count+1;

float aa=(M1/count);

System.out.println("EA =" +aa);

request.setAttribute("EA", aa); }

else if(num[as] <=8 && num[as]>=10)

{ count1=count1+1;

a = (a4 / count1);

System.out.println("EB =" +a);

request.setAttribute("EB", a);

} else if(num[as] <=6 && num[as]>=10)

{ count2=count2+1;

float a11 = (a1/count2);

System.out.println("PR =" +a11);
```

```
request.setAttribute("PR", a11);

} else if(num[as] <=6 && num[as]>=10)

{ count3=count3+1;

float a32=a6/count3;

System.out.println("RA =" +a32);

request.setAttribute("RA", a32);

} Else

{ System.out.println("No Allocation");

request.setAttribute("NO", "No Allocation");

} System.out.println("array"+num[as]);

}RequestDispatcher
rd=request.getRequestDispatcher(com.budget.web.controller.frontcontroller.s_scheme);

rd.forward(request,response); }

}
```

Percentage Growth Rate Calculation

```
package com.budget.web.utility;

import java.io.IOException;

import java.io.PrintWriter;

import javax.servlet.RequestDispatcher;

import javax.servlet.ServletException;

import javax.servlet.annotation.WebServlet;

import javax.servlet.http.HttpServlet;

import javax.servlet.http.HttpServletRequest;

import javax.servlet.http.HttpServletResponse;

import com.budget.web.model.fundtable;

/**
```

```
* Servlet implementation class GrowthRatePercentage

*/

@WebServlet("/GrowthRatePercentage")

public class GrowthRatePercentage extends HttpServlet {

private static final long serialVersionUID = 1L;

/**

* @see HttpServlet#HttpServlet()

*/

public GrowthRatePercentage() {

super();

// TODO Auto-generated constructor stub

}

protected void doPost(HttpServletRequest request, HttpServletResponse response) throws
ServletException, IOException {

fundtable ti=new fundtable();

ti.setpresent_year(request.getParameter(com.budget.web.controller.frontcontroller.P_present_
year));

ti.setlast_year(request.getParameter(com.budget.web.controller.frontcontroller.L_last_year));

ti.setnumber_of_year(request.getParameter(com.budget.web.controller.frontcontroller.N_num
ber_of_year));

response.setContentType("text/html");

PrintWriter out = response.getWriter();

out.print("<a href=\"home.jsp>");

System.out.println("YOUR APPLICATION HAS BEEN SAVED ");

check(ti,request,response);

}

public void check(fundtable ti,HttpServletRequest request,HttpServletResponse response)
throws IOException, ServletException
```

```
{
String present=null;
String last=null;
String year=null;
float growth_rate;
float a,b,d,Percentage_Rate,Annual_Percent;
try
{
present = ti.getpresent_year();
last= ti.getlast_year();
year= ti.getnumber_of_year();
a= ((Float.parseFloat(present))-(Float.parseFloat(last)));
Percentage_Rate=((a/(Float.parseFloat(last)))*100);
//b=1/(Float.parseFloat(year));
//d=(float) Math.pow(a,b);
//growth_rate=(d-1);
System.out.println("Percent Rate =" +Percentage_Rate);
request.setAttribute("Percentage_rate", Percentage_Rate);
//Annual Percentage
Annual_Percent=(Percentage_Rate/Float.parseFloat(year));
//float growth_rate_perct=growth_rate*100;
System.out.println("Annual_Percent =" +Annual_Percent);
request.setAttribute("Annual_Percent",Annual_Percent);
// for next year money increment
float Incremental_Budget= (((Float.parseFloat(present))*Annual_Percent)/100);
System.out.println("Incremental_Budget =" +Incremental_Budget);
```

```
request.setAttribute("Incremental_Budget",Incremental_Budget);

float Budget_Allocation=Incremental_Budget+(Float.parseFloat(present));

System.out.println("Budget_Allocation="+Budget_Allocation);

request.setAttribute("Budget_Allocation",Budget_Allocation);

RequestDispatcher
rd=request.getRequestDispatcher(com.budget.web.controller.frontcontroller.G_Growth_Perce
nt);

rd.forward(request,response);

}

catch(Exception s)

{

System.out.println(s);

}} }
```

APPENDIX C

BUDGET ALLOCATION USING GENETIC ALGORITHM APPROACH FITNESS CALCULATION

```
public class FitnessCalc

{

static byte[] solution = new byte[9900];

public static void setSolution(byte[] newSolution)

{

solution = newSolution;

}

static void setSolution(String newSolution) {

solution = new byte[newSolution.length()];

for (int i = 0; i < newSolution.length(); i++) {

String character = newSolution.substring(i, i + 1);

if (character.contains("0") || character.contains("1")) {

solution[i] = Byte.parseByte(character);

} else

{

solution[i] = 0;

}}}

static int getFitness(Individual individual)

{

int fitness = 0;

for (int i = 100; i < individual.size() && i < solution.length; i++) {

if (individual.getGene(i) == solution[i]) {

fitness++;
```

```
}

}

return fitness;

}

static int getMaxFitness() {

int maxFitness = solution.length;

return maxFitness;

}

}
```

GA Algorithm

```
public class Algorithm

{

private static final double uniformRate = 0.8;

private static final double mutationRate = 0.02;

private static final int tournamentSize = 5;

private static final boolean elitism = true;

public static Population evolvePopulation(Population pop)

{

Population newPopulation = new Population(pop.size(), false);

if (elitism)

{

newPopulation.saveIndividual(0, pop.getFittest());

}

int elitismOffset;

if (elitism)

{
```

```
elitismOffset = 1;

}

else

{

elitismOffset = 0;

}

for (int i = elitismOffset; i < pop.size(); i++) {

Individual indiv1 = tournamentSelection(pop);

Individual indiv2 = tournamentSelection(pop);

Individual newIndiv = crossover(indiv1, indiv2);

newPopulation.saveIndividual(i, newIndiv);

}

for (int i = elitismOffset; i < newPopulation.size(); i++) {

mutate(newPopulation.getIndividual(i));

}

return newPopulation;

}

private static Individual crossover(Individual indiv1, Individual indiv2) {

Individual newSol = new Individual();

for (int i = 0; i < indiv1.size(); i++) {

if (Math.random() <= uniformRate) {

newSol.setGene(i, indiv1.getGene(i));

} else {

newSol.setGene(i, indiv2.getGene(i));

}

}
```

```
return newSol;

}
```

GA Population Selection

```
private static void mutate(Individual indiv) {

for (int i = 0; i < indiv.size(); i++) {

if (Math.random() <= mutationRate) {

byte gene = (byte) Math.round(Math.random());

indiv.setGene(i, gene);

}}}

private static Individual tournamentSelection(Population pop) {

Population tournament = new Population(tournamentSize, false);

for (int i = 0; i < tournamentSize; i++) {

int randomId = (int) (Math.random() * pop.size());

tournament.saveIndividual(i, pop.getIndividual(randomId));

}

Individual fittest = tournament.getFittest();

return fittest;

}

}

Algorithm for Individual Selection

public class Individual

{

static int defaultGeneLength = 14000;

private byte[] genes = new byte[defaultGeneLength];

private int fitness = 0;

public void generateIndividual() {
```

```java
for (int i = 0; i < size(); i++) {

byte gene = (byte) Math.round(Math.random());

genes[i] = gene;

}}

public static void setDefaultGeneLength(int length) {

defaultGeneLength = length;

}

public byte getGene(int index) {

return genes[index];

}

public void setGene(int index, byte value) {

genes[index] = value;

fitness = 0;

}

public int size() {

return genes.length;

}

public int getFitness() {

if (fitness == 0) {

fitness = FitnessCalc.getFitness(this);

}

return fitness;

}

@Override

public String toString() {

String geneString = "";
```

```
for (int i = 0; i < size(); i++) {

geneString += getGene(i);

}

return geneString;

}

}
```

Chart Preparation

```
public class chart extends HttpServlet

{

public chart() {

super();

}

protected void doGet(HttpServletRequest request, HttpServletResponse response) throws ServletException, IOException

{

}

protected void doPost(HttpServletRequest request, HttpServletResponse response) throws ServletException, IOException

{

fundtable ti=new fundtable();

ti.setpresent_year(request.getParameter(com.budget.web.controller.frontcontroller.N_Ncert));

response.setContentType("text/html");

PrintWriter out = response.getWriter();

out.print("<a href=\"home.jsp>");

System.out.println("YOUR APPLICATION HAS BEEN SAVED ");

check(ti,request,response);

}
```

```
public void check(fundtable ti,HttpServletRequest request,HttpServletResponse response)
throws IOException, ServletException

{

String year=null;

String amount=null;

try

{

String driverName = "oracle.jdbc.driver.OracleDriver";

Class.forName(driverName);

{

Properties pro=new Properties();

InputStream in = this.getClass().getClassLoader().getResourceAsStream("config.properties");

pro.load(in);

String serverName = pro.getProperty("server");

String portNumber = pro.getProperty("port");

String sid = pro.getProperty("sid");

String url = "jdbc:oracle:thin:@" + serverName + ":" + portNumber + ":" + sid;

String username = pro.getProperty("user");

String password = pro.getProperty("password");

Connection conn = DriverManager.getConnection(url, username, password);

Statement st = conn.createStatement();

String sql = "select * from ncert";

System.out.println(sql);

ResultSet rs=st.executeQuery(sql);

ArrayList<Table> T=new ArrayList<Table>();

while(rs.next())
```

```
{

Table T1= new Table();

T1.year=rs.getString("year");

T1.amount=rs.getString("amount");

T.add(T1);

}

request.setAttribute("Table", T);

conn.close();

RequestDispatcher
rd=request.getRequestDispatcher(com.budget.web.controller.frontcontroller.f_fund);

rd.forward(request,response);

}} catch(Exception s)

{ System.out.println(s);

}}}
```

Java Bean for Mean Calculation

```
public class mean

{

String
year_2009,year_2010,year_2011,year_2012,year_2013,year_2014,year_2015,number_of_year;

public mean()

{

year_2009=null;

year_2010=null;

year_2011=null;

year_2012=null;

year_2013=null;
```

```
year_2014=null;

year_2015=null;

number_of_year=null;

}

public void setyear_2009(String s) {

this.year_2009=s;

}

public String getyear_2009() {

return year_2009;

}

public void setyear_2010(String s) {

this.year_2010=s;

}

public String getyear_2010() {

return year_2010;

}

public void setyear_2011(String s) {

this.year_2011=s;

}

public String getyear_2011() {

return year_2011;

}

public void setyear_2012(String s) {

this.year_2012=s;

}

public String getyear_2012() {
```

```
return year_2012;

}

public void setyear_2013(String s) {

this.year_2013=s;

}

public String getyear_2013() {

return year_2013;

}

public void setyear_2014(String s) {

this.year_2014=s;

}

public String getyear_2014() {

return year_2014;

}

public void setyear_2015(String s) {

this.year_2015=s;

}

public String getyear_2015() {

return year_2015;

}

public void setnumber_of_year(String s) {

this.number_of_year=s;

}

public String getnumber_of_year() {

return number_of_year;

}}
```

Java Bean for Growth Rate Calculation

```java
public class Growth_Rate {

String present_year,last_year,number_of_year,ncert;

public Growth_Rate ()

{

present_year=null;

last_year=null;

number_of_year=null;

ncert=null;

} public void setpresent_year(String s) {

this.present_year=s;

} public String getpresent_year() {

return present_year;

}

public void setlast_year(String s) {

this.last_year=s;

}

public String getlast_year() {

return last_year;

}

public void setnumber_of_year(String s) {

this.number_of_year=s;

}

public String getnumber_of_year() {

return number_of_year;

}
```

```
public void setncert(String s) {

this.ncert=s;

}

public String getncert() {

return ncert;

}}
```

LIST OF ABBREVIATIONS

Glossary

OCBA Optimal Computing Budget Allocation

EA Equal Allocation

GA Genetic Algorithm

GR Growth Rate

PGR Percent Growth Rate

SSA Sum Squared Accuracy

MSA Mean Squared Accuracy

PCS Probability of Correct Selection

SUBJECT INDEX

www.ingramcontent.com/pod-product-compliance
Lightning Source LLC
Chambersburg PA
CBHW041429050326
40690CB00002B/471